An alternative view o

*The Dedalus Book of
Medieval Literature:
the Grin of the Gargoyle*

The Dedalus Book of Medieval Literature: the Grin of the Gargoyle

Edited and translated by
Brian Murdoch

Dedalus

Eastern Arts
Board Funded

Published in the UK by Dedalus Ltd, Langford Lodge, St Judith's Lane, Sawtry, Cambs, PE17 5XE

UK ISBN 1 873982 02 X

Distributed in Australia & New Zealand by Peribo Pty Ltd, 58 Beaumont Road, Mount Kuring- gai N.S.W. 2080

Distributed in Canada by Marginal Distribution, Unit 102, 277, George Street North, Peterborough, Ontario, KJ9 3G9

First published by Dedalus in 1995
Compilation, Introduction & Notes copyright © Brian Murdoch 1995
Translation copyright © Dedalus 1995

Printed in Finland by Wsoy
Typeset by Datix International Limited, Bungay, Suffolk

For Jon and Máire West

THE EDITOR/TRANSLATOR

Brian Murdoch is Professor of German at the University of Stirling and a former Visiting Fellow of Trinity Hall, Cambridge, and of Magdalen College, Oxford, where he delivered the Waynflete Lectures in 1994. Primarily a specialist in medieval and renaissance literature (German, Latin, Celtic), he has also written on the literature of the world wars, and has translated classical and medieval Latin as well as medieval and modern German texts. He collaborated with his son, Adrian Murdoch, in translating material for Geoffrey Farrington's *Dedalus Book of Roman Decadence.*

PREFACE

Anthologies are always a matter of luck, and there ought to be a formula of apology for not having included somebody's favourite. But the selection depends, like it or not, on the taste, knowledge and competence of the anthologist/translator. Indeed, for a number of reasons I have had to leave out various interesting figures altogether: Vlad the Impaler, for example, and Torquemada, and any number of dubious medieval popes (with, in the case of the Borgias at least, many of their relatives). On the other hand, I have also had to omit the Anglo-Saxon queen Aelfthryth, interesting not only on the grounds of her impossible name, nor because she was the mother of Ethelred the Unready (neither of which she could really help), but for her connivance at the murder of her stepson Edward the Martyr at Corfe Castle in 878.

A couple of general points *do* need to be made, however. The first is that the Middle Ages were well aware of how fallen mankind is anyway, and decay can be political, physical or moral. The second is that very familiar material has been left out: Chaucer and most of Boccaccio are absent. Against that, it is hoped that some of the less well-known pieces included will be of interest, such as the German poem of *Helmbrecht,* about a young man who leaves his farm to join a robber baron. A lack of background knowledge and linguistic competence has led to the absence of Iberian or Slav materials. Beyond that, the anthology tries to cover as broad a field as possible within an interpretation of 'medieval' that runs from the fall of Rome to the Reformation. A lot of the material is in verse, it is true, but this reflects the state of affairs in medieval writing, especially writing for entertainment.

The extract from *Waltharius* is from my own full translation: *Walthari* (Glasgow, 1989), and I am grateful to Mark

Ward, my fellow-editor of the series *Scottish Papers in Germanic Studies,* for permission to reprint.

Brian Murdoch   Stirling, September 1994

CONTENTS

INTRODUCTION:
FALLEN MAN

When the Vikings sacked Northumbria at the end of the eighth century, one famous northerner, Alcuin, who had left York for a high-level administrative post in Charlemagne's European Community some years earlier, was not particularly surprised. God was clearly punishing the people of Northumbria for their decadence, and more specifically for their propensity to thieving and fornication. Alcuin wrote to the King of Northumbria and told him so. The monks of Lindisfarne, too, had obviously brought it on themselves; they had not been spending enough time on spiritual reading, but had been enjoying heroic tales instead, and if the tales as such were hardly decadent, reading them *was*, especially when one should really be reading more improving works (and it would be more than churlish to add: 'like Alcuin's biblical commentaries'). 'What,' asked Alcuin sniffily, 'has some Germanic hero got to do with Christ?' It wasn't a particularly original remark. Several centuries earlier, St Jerome had asked roughly the same thing about the reading of Vergil instead of the Bible, and a few centuries in the other direction, Martin Luther would ask it again. More pragmatically, Luther provided some thoroughly militaristic hymns as a counter to the popular songs that were so very – well, *popular*. We, on the other hand, might be more inclined to ask a slightly different question to that posed by Alcuin: when were the Middle Ages? They are called the Middle Ages, of course, on account of their coming at the beginning, but beyond that no-one is ever sure, and to be on the safe side, we have to adopt some kind of formula like 'from the fall of the Roman Empire to the Reformation,' which covers well over a thousand years, giving plenty of time for whole empires to rise from nothing and descend again into decadence, usually, though not always passing through a stage of civilisation on the way.

The Middle Ages are, however, in the popular mind at least, still centuries either of piety and courtesy, or of superstitious but vigorous thuggery. The first view calls up hairshirts and monasteries on the one hand, and genteel interpersonal behaviour in a fantasy world on the other, with ladies out of reach on pedestals, and knights with their anachronistic plate-armour and their well-controlled libidos quite untarnished, either pining in love, or out scouring the countryside for the Holy Grail. The second view is rather simpler: back in the mists of medieval ignorance (it runs) warriors or groups of warriors (usually Germanic) took great delight in killing things, either dragons, monsters, or (most often) each other, but always for the sake of gold or power or just ordinary fame, because after the event, the survivors would all go to the mead-hall, drink a great deal, and sing heroic songs about killing things. The Middle Ages, then, is a time of thugs or wimps, but neither, on the face of it, seem to have much to do with actual decadence, with the degeneration of a society (or parts of it) into softened luxury and a studied concentration on sexual and physical delights, or with the kind of abuse of power and position which can in its turn lead to the complete collapse of that society. Popular views of the Middle Ages (Sir Walter Scott, Wagner and Hollywood all have a great deal to answer for) do contain a few elements of truth, but they do not take into account that falling into sin is *always* a possibility, always the other side of the coin of civilisation. The Middle Ages were more acutely aware of this than many another period.

Medieval Christianity was preoccupied with Adam and Eve, and it was generally reckoned that the first fall predisposed mankind to a state of permanent sinfulness. Medieval theologians, in fact, presupposed a fall prior to that of Adam and Eve, that of Lucifer and his associates, the rebel angels who came to populate hell. In medieval drama, much is made of devils, who parody Christian ritual, mock the Lord's Prayer, and say things (as a devil expostulates in a late medieval Swiss play) like '*Botz hosenlatz und nestelglimpff,*' a finesounding phrase which avoids a direct blasphemy on the

14

name of God, and means something like 'Odds codpieces and dangly bits.' It is a nice irony that medieval plays often had small boys (a major repository for and surely the best evidence we have for the existence of original sin) playing the many demons that provided light relief. Nevertheless, for the Middle Ages Adam and Eve were our very real progenitors (Noah took apes onto the Ark, but not as revered ancestors), and their fall has a lasting effect on us all. Admittedly, the presentation of it had to be adapted sometimes to put the blame more firmly on Eve, but all their descendants were deemed to bear the traces of that first disobedience. At the same time, the medieval Christian was told to keep the story of Adam and Eve firmly in mind as a warning not to do what they predisposed him to do anyway. Just as the devil tempted Eve, so too he could tempt anyone. In fact, every bit of the Bible could be used as a warning, and because decadence set in almost at once (murderous Cain, bigamous Lamech, the presumptuous builders of Babel, the wicked generation drowned in the flood), the lapses of the patriarchs are often used to warn against moral decay. Here is St Jerome again, in a letter about Noah's drunkenness. Though it was probably designed for the wider audience of posterity, it is ostensibly addressed to a girl who was fifteen at the time and who would become his secretary later. Noah's experiment with strong drink, it will be recalled, led to his involuntarily exposing himself. 'After Noah's drunkenness came the uncovering of his thighs,' says Jerome. 'Lust joins indulgence. First the belly swells, then other organs.' One supposes that the recipient of the letter knew what he was on about.

In general terms we can distinguish between moral, religious and physical (or perhaps architectural) decay, as well as social-political decadence. The first (and most universal) of these categories speaks for itself, and medieval writers responded to over-indulgence, wild behaviour and sexual excess in various ways, ranging from homiletic thundering through mild (or mildly hypocritical) regret, down to a gleeful hedonism that was not always ironic, though it certainly could be. Sermons warn in great detail about sins, and so do confessional handbooks, many of which demand the confession of sins that one might not even have *thought* of without consulting the handbook in the first place. St Jerome's words of warning to the young lady had their echoes in textbooks of behaviour, either designed for the clergy or nuns, or just as etiquette-books aimed in particular at youth, in whom the force of original sin was indeed felt to be particularly vigorous. Excesses of drinking and of gambling loom large as poetic themes, though the regret expressed in these works is often regret at not having enough cash to indulge in the activities. Just as frequently, we get a defiant jollity in writings about wine and song, and it is very often there, too, in literature about the third element of the triad, women, who are sometimes treated far more equally than one might expect. Marie de France's adulterers in *King Equitan* both get their come-uppance, but both ladies and gentlemen are equally pro-active in the sexual sphere in medieval narratives. The simple choreography of some of the tales – Chaucer's *Reeve's Tale* is probably the neatest example – implies actual delight in the less than moral. That story involves a medieval bedroom (and medieval nights were darker than ours, without background light of any description) containing three beds. One contains a miller and his wife, with a cradle at the end. The next contains the nubile daughter, the third two male students. During the night, student A hops into bed with nubile daughter. Student B is disgruntled, so waits until the miller's wife goes out to relieve herself, and moves the cradle to the end of *his* bed, to which the miller's wife then returns. Eventually student A leaves the daughter, avoids the bed with the cradle, assumes that the now solo miller is actually student B, and tells him what he has been doing. All hell then breaks loose. There are plenty of tales like this in other languages (some requiring a fairish suspension of disbelief) but the delight is always there. Not, of course, that honest rumpy-pumpy is especially wicked. The Church thought it was, though, and there *can* be an edge, even with the most innocently comic description of well-choreographed sex.

Alternative attitudes to religion abound in the Middle

Ages, even though the whole period is often seen as the age of piety. In some ways, of course, it *was* an age of saints, but for all that, excessive piety probably always leads to the opposite, and certainly the monastic orders went through a regular cycle of decadence and toughening-up throughout the Middle Ages. Most of the new monastic orders came about because their ascetic founders thought that monasticism thus far had become too lax. The same principle, writ large, also underlies the Reformation, at the end of the period, when accusations of decadence fly in all directions. Nor was it long before the Reformers started accusing each other of laxity and splitting up, and within the Catholic Church after the Council of Trent had sorted out some of their own problems, new orders continued to arise.

Even asceticism can go too far, though, and the Middle Ages knew that, too. There is a Latin poem about a holy man who desperately wanted to be a saint, and had to be locked outside and told to live off 'the food of the angels' before he realised that he was going a bit too far, and did actually need a meal. More humble priests are a common target in literature, too, though this has something to do with the fact that they were simply more familiar to the Middle Ages than to us. At the beginning of the present century, G. G. Coulton, a notable medieval historian who nevertheless spent perhaps rather too much of his time attacking exaggerated notions of universal piety (and going for the throat of Hilaire Belloc in particular) drew attention in an entertaining paper called 'The Monastic Legend' to the case of William de Bittendene, of St James' Priory near Exeter, who was noted in the fourteenth century as being 'oftentimes convicted of embezzlement and fornication.' He would have been punished had the bishop been able to catch him, but he couldn't, and William crops up again, still Prior, and apparently still dissolute, a year or so later, this time in trouble for not paying taxes. Coulton also cites the case of another Prior, 'found in gross misconduct at eleven o'clock on a Friday in Lent.' When Bishop Alcock wound up the nunnery of St Radegund in Cambridge at the end of the fifteenth century, to turn it into

17

Jesus College, he noted that there were only a couple of nuns left, and one of those had a somewhat dubious reputation; later still, the activities of some of the more notorious Popes (who were still patrons of the arts, we must not forget) are well documented. These things have to be relativised, of course. But whatever the actual *extent* of clerical misdeeds really was (and let us be fair: perusal of some Sunday tabloids might well distort one's views somewhat on the twentieth-century English vicar), satirical stories involving oversexed priests make good reading. The same strain of what looks like gleeful irreligiousness is visible in the somewhat surprising fact that most of the liturgy was the target of parody in the Middle Ages. Actually, most of things learned at school were subject to parody; a medieval 'erotic grammar' makes a great deal of the copulative, but the religious parodies *are* striking. There is a Latin 'monetary Gospel' written, prophetically enough, in Germany, while boozy imitations of the Psalms, and of the whole Mass, are also known. Mock sermons include a rude parody of a homily on Adam and Eve which, in a way, proves the point about original sin by stressing their delight in original sex. It is honestly dirty, and not remotely pornographic, and when the world population was exactly two, surely most sex was original. And none of these things are *really* irreligious, just irreverent. The parodies are simply the literary equivalents of the grinning and sometimes vulgar gargoyles on the cathedral roof. They don't detract from the sweep of the whole thing, but they do serve a useful deflecting function, and they are often funny in themselves. Their downstairs equivalents, equally jolly but not usually as vulgar, are the carvings you find on bench-ends in the older cathedrals. Writings on morals and religion in the Middle Ages vary, of course, and the reaction to man's intrinsically fallen state can either be thundering disapproval, awful warnings, stories of nick-of-time rescues (with the implication that you, the audience, might not be so lucky), right down to a giggling awareness that everyone – even the supposed moral guardians – enjoys a little excess now and again. When it has all gone, and the would-be profligate is unfortunately

18

past it, however, nostalgia and anger remain in about equal measure, and there is a poignant expression of this in the number of poems (not just medieval ones) which reminisce on the personal level about sex and drinking (well, mostly sex) no longer being what they used to be.

Empires do not last, and the Roman empire, which had been characterised by fine stone buildings, declined pretty visibly, and those who came after watched this and commented on it, again sometimes with nostalgia, although much of what the Romans built was helped on its way; the magnificent basilica of Constantine in Trier, in Germany, has been knocked down and rebuilt with a positively monotonous regularity by different Germanic tribes since the Romans put it up, possibly because it is too large for any passing attacker to miss. Sadly, Allied bombers got it last, but it is up again. Societies can crumble all too easily as well, however, usually in the wake of weak leadership, or perhaps with a leadership that isn't able to cope with the size of the organisation. Medieval society (if such a generalisation is possible) could be precarious. A very conservative German poet – a commoner called Konrad of Würzburg – wrote in the thirteenth century a little story designed to show that chivalry and honest knightly bravery are Good Things, even if they were, in his day, in somewhat short supply. In his tale, the eponymous Henry of Kempten leaps out of a bath, grabs a sword, and, though naked, saves the life of the Holy Roman Emperor, from whom he had become estranged. All well and good, but the underlying political sense of the story is in the reason *why* he was estranged. He had been attending a ceremonial and civilised feast in the Emperor's presence with all the other knights (or more accurately: with all the other tough, independent, bloody-minded noblemen). One of his pages absent-mindedly eats a piece of bread before grace, the Emperor's chamberlain clouts the lad and draws blood, Henry of Kempten knocks the chamberlain down and kills him, and when the Emperor demands punishment for Henry, the latter grabs the Emperor by the beard, points a sword (why was he armed at a formal feast?) at his throat and

19

demands safe passage away from the court. It is true that there is a story-book reconciliation after Henry has saved the Emperor, but what Konrad of Würzburg is really saying is: 'look, the feudal system is all very fine, but it would not take very much at all to bring the whole lot down about our ears.' And he was right. The Holy Roman Empire collapsed into social chaos and a welter of private armies not long after.

Getting a strong leader was a matter of luck, and usually temporary. In England Henry II sorted out the mess left by Stephen (so we can forgive Henry's private indiscretions, perhaps, with Rosamund de Clifford), but his successor, Richard, is questionable, and so on. In medieval writings we often encounter a kind of desperate conservatism as a response to potential anarchy. One of the rhetorical set-pieces that the Middle Ages liked, and which is another sign of their awareness of man's fallen state, was summed up with the Latin tagname *laudatio temporis actii*, 'praise of the good old days.' Whether they ever *were* good is as much a matter of debate as how brave the new world has become. Even with a strong leader we are likely to be faced with another celebrated historical truism: that power corrupts, and absolute power corrupts absolutely. The Roman world produced its share of examples, and so did the Middle Ages, men and women alike, in spite of the way that 'great figures of the Middle Ages' – like Charlemagne, for example – have always been presented.

In their writings, medieval historians, clerics, satirists and especially poets show us over and over again that man is by nature corruptible, at least, although it was never a matter of despair. If you were wicked, you would get your just deserts eventually. Our own views of the Middle Ages may vary. Do we see the period as the Victorian genre painters did, with the lady in the long white frock and eccentric headgear, on a perfectly genuine pedestal, presenting a chaplet to a knight in improbably shining armour? Or do we revise our *Boy's Book of Heroes* view of Richard Lionheart to see him as a greedy, self-centred, politically incompetent thug with unclear sexual habits? It would be impossible to pigeon-hole, to categorise the whole period anyway, even if we could decide when the

Middle Ages actually *were*. Nevertheless, although books on the Middle Ages tend to show, as evidence of the onward march of civilisation, photographs of massive Gothic cathedrals, they are not often in close-up. If they were, you would be able to see the gargoyles better.

One such cathedral has a gargoyle of a demon, grinning at you over his shoulder, whilst displaying his bare bottom, from which the rainwater falls from a great height. It's a salutary comment on fallen humanity.

PROLOGUE: ORIGINAL SINS

The Middle Ages had in front of them the ultimate – or to
be more accurate, the very *first* – example of a sin, that of
Adam, who was at the same time the genetic reason for
everyone's predisposition to sinfulness. He was also a ghastly
warning to his descendants. The fall of Adam and Eve was
entirely real to the times: Darwin, Freud, and for that matter
Milton, are all a good way off. However, it was left for
Adam's progeny to sort out the nice distinctions between
original sin, original sinfulness, *the* original sin, and (just
occasionally) *an* original sin. Here are two approaches, one
desperately serious, and another that starts off in a familiar
manner, but degenerates somewhat, rather proving the point
about predisposition to sin. The first is a brief but very much
quoted interpretation of the fall of man by Gregory I, Pope,
principal pastoral theologian of the Middle Ages, and eventually a saint. He lived from about 540 to 604, and reputedly
arranged for the conversion of England with a joke about
Angles and angels.

Gregory the Great

Moral Lessons from the Book of Job IV, 27

There are four stages by which sin is perpetrated in the heart, and four in which it is actually put into practice. In the heart, these stages are: suggestion, delight, consent, and brazening-it-out. In practice, the suggestion comes from the Old Enemy, delight from the flesh, consent from the spirit, and brazen self-justification from a general over-confidence in the self . . . Now, the serpent made the persuasive suggestion, Eve delighted in it, Adam consented, and when he was called upon to confess his guilt, he brazenly denied it. And, I do assure you, all this happens with mankind every day, the very same things experienced by our first natural parents. The serpent did the persuading, just as now the Old Enemy secretly makes evil suggestions to mankind. Eve delighted in it, just as the sensual flesh gives way to pleasure when it hears the old serpent's words. Adam consented to what the woman put to him, just as, once the flesh has been seized with delight, the weak spirit then bends towards it. And when he was required by God to confess his guilt, Adam would not do so, just as the spirit, turned from the true path by sin, becomes – to its own ruin! – hardened by brazen audacity.

This anonymous German poem is the very first piece in a large collective manuscript from the early fifteenth century, now in Karlsruhe. One wonders whether the compiler of the collection had read past the first dozen lines, which are disarmingly orthodox-looking. Anyway, fully (and completely spuriously) supported by Biblical quotations, Adam develops preoccupations here which have absolutely nothing to do with scrumping, and the medieval German word *kunterlin* (translated here as 'pussy') genuinely *does* mean (also) 'a little furry animal.' The ending is nicely ambiguous.

Adam and Eve

IN THE BEGINNING GOD CREATED HEAVEN AND EARTH

> Dearly beloved, for today
> the text on which I want to say
> a few words, really does begin
> the Scriptures (although in Latin).
> Now you, each woman and each man,
> should say 'Our Fathers' when you can,
> and an 'Ave Maria' too,
> so that, through God's great mercy, you
> may all experience as well
> the things that I've a mind to tell.
>
> In the beginning, then, God's hand
> made air, fire, water and the land –
> the 'elements' we call these four,
> from which, now and for evermore
> all things are created – at least
> that's what we're all told by the priests.
> And God created after this
> the angels in their heavenly bliss,
> of which one was an angel fair

who bore the name of Lucifer.
He coveted the holy crown,
and afterwards he was cast down
because of his great sin of pride,
to hell's abyss, there to reside.

After that fall, God straight away
made man upon the earth to stay;
He wanted humankind for sure
to live on earth for evermore.

Now when God had created man,
the name He gave him was 'Adam,'
a name that God Himself thought fit.
He took a rib and fashioned it
into a woman, and when done
He said: 'You two shall be as one,
and shall increase upon the earth,
and all your kin shall show their worth.
What joined together is by me,
shall never put asunder be.'
The next thing God wanted to do
was breathe His life into the two.
Adam stood up, began to move,
and God put in him thoughts of love,
made him behave as if, that time,
Adam was thirty, in his prime,
and he behaved accordingly.
I'm telling all this honestly!
These were his words, I do believe,
when first he laid his eyes on Eve:
'My bones and flesh the Lord did take
so that He could a woman make.'
Then Adam added something new
(which instinct prompted him to do).
He pointed with his finger where
the short and brown and curly hair
is seen above a woman's thighs.

On this he set adoring eyes –
the little pussy pleased him so.
He said with passion: 'Eve, I know,
because of this sweet little place,
man will part from his parents' grace,
and to his wife will wish to cleave,
because of pussy, and not leave.
It's in the Book – I shan't deceive!

THEREFORE SHALL A MAN LEAVE HIS FATHER AND HIS MOTHER,
AND SHALL CLEAVE UNTO HIS WIFE ETC.

We read that Adam only sinned
the once, and only in one thing –
he took the apple, and he bit,
and very much regretted it,
and undertook a great penance
to clear his disobedience.
But nowhere will you find at all
that sex was ever culpable,
nor was it ever deemed a vice
to cause the loss of Paradise –
such nonsense never could be thought!
How could mankind enjoy as sport
something seen as a mortal sin?
Now, evidence may be found in
the letters of St Paul, a saint
of holiness beyond complaint.
He was a teacher, widely read,
so we must mark his words. He said
that loving isn't sin at all,
He says, the holy man St. Paul,
in an epistle, in Latin
(the language I shall cite it in):

27

'It's best to wed and get a bit,
than be on fire for lack of it!'
The commentaries add this gloss:
'Girls, if in thoughts of sex you're lost
so you can't serve God properly,
nor concentrate wholeheartedly,
then always *give in* to the man
who occupies your thoughts. You can,
by doing so, remove all stress,
and pray again, your mind at rest.
Whatever you desire of God
it shall be granted by His word.
Now, young women, take notice all:
first, make yourselves look beautiful
then go and find yourselves a man
and take the best advice I can
give you. And if the monks should say
that you should rather turn away,
then to their strictures pay no heed,
to follow them there is no need.
They have one thought, and only one:
that you should service them alone!
But listen if your monk should say:
he's not sinned who with women lay.
Of course there is no doubt of it
that you can't sin a little bit
if you leave women totally.
But still he's wrong as wrong can be
if he says it's a mortal sin
(I mean it!) to enjoy women.
I'll tell you something else as well.
Men won't be heading straight for hell
if they should bed a woman for
the usual night-time sports and more.
I say all this and know it's true
because that's in the Bible, too.

You'll find it in Isaiah IV
that seven women battled for
a single man – it's so, I swear,
without a lie, it tells us there.

Now the sermon is at an end
and for your souls I you commend
that you get on your knees and pray
and one act of contrition say.'

'I've been a naughty girl, alas,
and I have been very remiss,
not giving men all that they ask.
To remedy that is my task.
That I've not let them go too far,
that I repent – *mea culpa*.
And furthermore I do confess
that I have frequently done less
than men wanted me to, and so
to do a penance I shall go,
and show my full contrition true.
Dear brother, now I ask of you,
your holiness, to absolve me,
and all the years I live, I'll see
that I do penance while I can
for having said 'no' to a man.
For if my body made him hot
I played the silly little clot;
and if he held my hand one day,
I quickly would snatch mine away;
and if he tried to fondle me,
I slapped his hand down off my knee.
And when he whispered in my ear,
far too often I would not hear.
But I'm a woman, and still young,
and my body is fit and strong,
so I can make up soon enough
for missing out on all that stuff.

I'm wiser than I used to be
so I shall furnish willingly
all I rejected in the past.
Whatever he shall of me ask,
whether his wants are big or small,
believe me, I shall fill them all.
Oh yes, this year I'm more mature –
whoever asks will get for sure
all that he wanted right away,
his heart's desire, this very day.
Yes, I'll do penance here below
to help my soul to heaven go;
may God His wings of grace unfurl
over a silly little girl.
And in God's name I'll work away
so one day He will let me say
that I've fulfilled all this and more
of what I missed out on before.
All things a man desires of me
twofold to him shall granted be;
I'll give it happily I know –
and even monks can have a go!
So now absolve me sir,' she said.
'I shall my dear. Right! Into bed!
The Lord pass down His mercy mild
upon your head, you naughty child,
and may He then your soul commend
to Paradise at your life's end.
For God sits there, the Trinity,
forever in His majesty,
and His law ever shall hold sway.'

That's it, that's all I've got to say.
If you've taken my sermon in,
and afterwards, for all your sin
made no contrition in your heart
and from your sins you will not part,
then to you I offer freely

a thousand days off Purgatory.

So you must say 'Amen' with me
to signal that you all agree.

Unoriginal Sins

Whenever the Church established itself in a new country (such as Germany in the eighth century), it provided lists of sins and formulas for confession, which presumably had the implicit instruction 'strike out those which do not apply.' They were based on the Ten Commandments and the Seven Deadly Sins, of course, but included quite a range. As warnings, here are two examples, one from a Latin list, the other from an early German *Form of Confession*. Some of the others have additional sins, like not paying tithes and taxes. These are the ones that lead directly to hell. The first list (the manuscript has handy translations of them into German, in fact) are probably not in order of importance (or preference), and the omissions in the second piece (from Würzburg) are not for the sake of propriety, but because of linguistic obscurity, though it *does* seem to cover pornography.

Two early Forms of Confession

These are the wicked sins by which the devil lures men down to hell:

> sins of the flesh
> false witness
> fornication
> avarice
> idolatry
> impurity
> bellicosity
> quarrelling
> jealousy
> anger
> brawling
> dissent
> wrangling
> envy

obstinacy
homicide
bullying
drunkenness
adultery
theft

Lord God Almighty, I confess to Thee and to the saints Thy companions, the sins which I have committed from the beginning in thought, word and deed: swearing, cursing, lying, talking nonsense; envy, hatred, lust and greed; unsavoury thoughts whilst asleep, turning my mind to things which are not allowed, lusts of the eye, the will and the ears ... I confess also to God that I have committed idolatry, theft, murder, excessive fornication both in the body and in the mind; I have coveted other men's goods; I have lied under oath and borne false witness ... I have committed unchaste things and sodomitic practices, polluted my body with unpermitted lusts, and gazed at things that I was not supposed to look upon ... I have gone against the Commandments in overeating, overdrinking until I vomited, in envy, hatred, lying ... and countless other sins ... many are my sins in thought, word and deed.

THE ROMAN EMPIRE GOES AND COMES

There is plenty of evidence for decadence in the lives of the Roman emperors, but the collapse of their empire was physical as well, with the great cities and fine roads crumbling and falling to pieces, something which the victorious barbarians could hardly fail to notice. Other empires came and went, some (like that of Attila the Hun) not lasting very long. Attila's successors – the next set of empire-builders – are the Franks, especially under Charlemagne, whose Frenchified name in English hides the fact that he was really German. He re-invented a Holy Roman Empire which wasn't any of those things. The Roman church – a far tougher survivor – was also a little variable, although a Pope (Leo III, whom Charlemagne had had to bail out once or twice) gave him imperial respectability when he crowned him. Charlemagne's biographer tried hard to make him into an Augustus, but didn't really succeed.

The fragmentary Anglo-Saxon poem known usually as 'The Ruin' (there is no title in the original) presents a picture of what happens after civilisation has gone beyond decay. The Saxons must have been impressed by the architecture of dead Roman cities like Bath – it is clearly the Roman bath-house (itself a symbol of decadence, perhaps?) which stayed in the mind. But this alliterative poem (a Germanic form far more rugged in itself than the elegant and careful hexameters of much Latin verse) makes the point about decadence and decay well because it avoids all overt censure or comment, without moralising about the good old days. Absence of noise also plays a big part here. The Anglo-Saxon poem is in the tenth-century Exeter Book, one of the great repositories of Anglo-Saxon texts.

The Ruin

Stone wall once well-wrought, now wrecked by fate,
city broken, the building-work of giants,
roofs caved, collapsed towers,
gates fallen, frost on the mortar,
houses harrowed, hollowed, shaking,
undermined by age. Earth's grip holds
the keen craftsmen, cold, long-dead,
in its hard hands; a hundred generations
went away. This wall, all mottled
with grey-red lichen outlived empires,
withstood storms till its steepness fell.
The walls crumble still, worn by weather . . .

[five fragmentary lines are omitted here]

One man's mind once made quick plans,
a rich man with many thoughts,
with iron he bound the braces of the walls.
There were bright halls, bath-houses aplenty,
raised roof-beams, and the roars of soldiers,
mead-halls without number, noisy with men,
till mighty fate made it all change.

Far and wide fell the plague-doomed,
death bore away the brave warriors,
their shrines and temples torn to the ground,
their city crushed. Cult-priests and soldiers
sank to earth. Thus every courtyard fell,
the roof shed its red tiles
from the great arch. All became ruin,
made into stone-mounds, where many men
gladhearted, gold-clad, gloriously once
drank down their wine with war-armour gleaming.
Treasures they saw, silver, diamonds,
jewels and riches, gemstones, too,
in this bright city of a broad empire.

36

Stone rooms were here, streams flowed,
giving great warmth; a good wall held
to its bright bosom those broad baths
of heated water (well-being for men!)
They let the hot streams . . .
gush forth on grey stones
. . . a round pool . . .
. . . there, where the baths were . . .
. . . a most noble thing . . .
. . . the city . . .

[Ironically the poem breaks down into a ruin itself, and only a few words can be made out in the last lines]

Attila's Hangover: the Eclipse of the Huns

Sometime between the ninth and the eleventh centuries (no-one is sure) a monk called Geraldus (about whom we know nothing) wrote (probably) a Latin poem of Walthari the Visigoth, who is taken as a hostage by Attila when the Hun empire is at the height of its power. Walthari becomes a great warrior, but after his fellow-hostage, the Frank, Hagano has escaped, Walthari and his Burgundian fiancée, Hildi-gunda (another hostage), hold a feast, get Attila very drunk, and make their escape with a lot of Attila's gold. To his distress (and that of his wife Ospirina) no-one will pursue Walthari, and the Huns fade out of the story. The whole thing is a literary reflection of the sudden collapse of the powerful Hun hegemony after the death of Attila, when it fell to Roman and Germanic forces. Attila reputedly died of a massive haemorrhage on his wedding-night, but here his fall is via the demon drink, an aspect of his reputation that Chaucer knew as well. The Franks ambushed Walthari on the way home.

Geraldus

Waltharius

(260–323 and 358–418)

                       Walthari whispered to the girl:
'You have been given charge of the royal coffers;
now listen well to what I have to say:
first take the king's helmet and his three-layered coat,
I mean the ringmail tunic with the mark of Wayland.
Then take two coffers – neither must be too large –
and fill them with arm-rings of Hunnish gold, until
you can barely lift the coffers up breast-high.
Procure for me four sets of footwear that will fit,
and then the same for you, and put them in the chests,
and this should fill them up completely. Secretly
get well-turned fish-hooks from the smith – we shall
want fish and birds for food when we are on our way,
and I shall be both fisherman and bird-trapper.
Do all these things within the week, but cautiously –
you know now all the things we need for our escape.
Now let me tell you how we shall begin our flight.
When the sun has crossed the heavens seven times,
for the king and queen, their vassals, lords and court
I shall prepare and give a splendid feast,
and make sure they all end in drunken sleep,
till not a single one knows what is happening.
But you must only take a small amount of wine
at table – do no more than merely quench your thirst.
When the others rise, then go about your tasks.
When the force of drink has conquered everyone
then we shall set off westwards with all speed.'
The maiden heard, and did all he had asked. And then
the day arrived for which the feast was planned. Walthari
had prepared a mighty feast of food and drink,
and luxury itself presided at his table.
When the king came into the tapestry-hung hall

the hero welcomed him with customary grace
and led him to a throne decked out with purple cloth.
Attila took his seat, and placed two noblemen
at right and left. A chamberlain arranged the rest
at table. A hundred guests were seated at that feast,
and ate dish after dish, and drank until they sweated.
One course was finished and another took its place,
as wonderful food steamed in its golden vessels
– for only gold appeared upon the linen cloth –
while Bacchus, god of wine, adorned the goblets
with sweet drinks that would tempt the taste of everyone.
Walthari urged them all to drink their fill.

The meal was over; now they left the table,
and the warrior said, laughing, to the king:
'With this, my lord, I beg, show us your favour,
let first yourself and then the others take their ease.'
And as he spoke he handed him a decorated cup
engraved with pictures of his ancestor's great deeds.
Attila took it and drained it at one draught,
and gave the order that the rest keep up with him.
The stewards came and went, and came, and served the wine,
brought brimming goblets and took empty ones away.
Attila and their host urged everybody on,
and very soon the whole hall was roaring drunk,
and inebriate babbling came from every mouth.
Great heroes – what a sight! – staggered on their feet.
Walthari, far into the night, kept bringing in
Bacchus' best, dissuading anyone who tried to leave,
until the power of drink and sleep overcame them all,
and there they lay – in doorways and in aisles.
Even if he had set fire to those walls,
there was not one who would have been aware of it.

[*Walthari and Hildigunda make their escape*]

The people of Attila's court, in sleep and wine
stayed where they lay until the following noon,
but once awake, they tried to find their general,

to thank him for the feast and offer him their praise.
Attila, with his aching head held in his hands,
came from his chamber, and in wretchedness called for
Walthari, so he could bemoan his sufferings.
His servants said that Walthari was nowhere to
be seen. The king, however, still assumed that he
would be in some dark, hidden nook that he had found
for himself, still sunk in a sound, unhearing sleep.

Then Ospirina noticed Hildigunda's absence.
Unusually, she failed to bring the queen her clothes.
The stricken Ospirina cried out to the king:
'A thousand curses on our feasting yesterday
and on the wine, the downfall of all the Huns!
What I foresaw and had already told the king
has now come true, and we shall not get over it.
The mainstay of your empire has given way today,
its power, support, and all its famous strength has gone.
Walthari, the jewel of the Huns, has fled,
and taken my dear and favoured Hildigunda.'

And now the king flared up in fearful rage,
as all his happiness gave way to heartache.
he tore his robe from his shoulders and threw it down,
his anguished mind filled with conflicting thoughts.
Just as the east wind churns up and drives the sands,
so was the king's mood, with wave on wave of sorrow,
his inner feelings turned this way and that, and what
went on inside him was reflected in his face,
although his anger would not let him say a word.
That whole day he would neither eat nor drink at all,
and his sorrows allowed his troubled mind no rest.
Night came, obscuring all the colours of the day,
the king fell on his bed, but never closed an eye,
tossing from side to side and from right to left,
feeling as if a spear had cut into his breast.
He started up, and tossed his head this way and that,
then sat bolt upright on his bed, a man distraught.

No help for it! He moved about within his fortress,
came back to bed, and then at once got up again,
and in that way he passed a long and sleepless night.

Meanwhile, the fleeing lovers hurried on, through
friendly silence, leaving the hated land behind.

Next day had barely dawned when Attila called in
his counsellors, and said: 'If anyone can bring
the fugitive Walthari, like a greyhound bitch,
in chains, I'll cover that man with pure gold
from every side when he stands before me, and as
I live I'll spread treasures on every path he treads.'

But there was no great warlord in all those lands,
no earl, no margrave, no baron and no knight
prepared, however much he wished to show his strength
and gain eternal glory for his bravery
(and fill his coffers with the rich rewards as well),
to try his hand against the anger of Walthari
and meet him face to face with a sword in his hand.
Walthari's strength was known, and all men knew too well
how many blows he gave, to win without a wound.

The king could not persuade a single warrior
to try for the rewards against odds like these.

Fredegonda, the Frankish Concubine

Roman Gaul eventually became the province of the Meroving-ian dynasty of Franks (the tribe who gave their name, eventu-ally, to France). This particular dynasty provided a range of interesting kings in the early Middle Ages; they claimed par-tial descent from a sea-monster (which, given some of their activities, seems pretty plausible), and their favourite political weapon appears to have been constructive homicide. One of the most spectacular *women* politicians of all time emerged at this period, and it is baffling that Fredegonda, first a concu-bine and then a queen, is not far better known than she is. Initially one of several concubines of the sixth-century King Chilperic, she manipulated him into removing his second wife, married him, and throughout the rest of her (all things considered, surprisingly long) life, showed consistent skill in the permanent removal of opponents. Not that she did it herself very often. Bishop Praetextatus of Rouen once sug-gested to her that she might be destined for hell, and finished up with a dagger in the ribs, although he wisely elected to die at his own altar rather than be treated by her doctors. One of the citizens of Rouen remonstrated with her after this, but she invited him to have a drink with her, and guess what happened? After the death of her husband in 584, Frede-gonda (who found time for several lovers whilst married to Chilperic) even managed to avoid being killed by Childebert II – she escaped by pleading pregnancy. Fredegonda's deeds colour the pages of Bishop (later Saint) Gregory of Tours' *History of the Franks*. Gregory lived from 539 to 594, and was made bishop in 573. His massive work is mostly a documenta-tion of his own times and the doings of the royal families, and it shows how very closely they followed many of the less salutary traditions of some of the Roman imperial families. The *History* is a little like *I, Claudius*, with Fredegonda as Livia. Chilperic was married first to Audovera and then to Galswintha, before he married Fredegonda, whom he prob-ably deserved. He had several children by his first wife, but they didn't survive. Of her own children, several died of various illnesses, and her usual reaction was to have someone else (sometimes rather a lot of people) killed, declaring it to have been their fault. Fredegonda herself died in 597. The two extracts show us first the demise of the unfortunate Galswintha, and then that of Clovis, Chilperic's son by Audovera, who was herself dragged from a convent and slaughtered on the orders of Fredegonda.

Gregory of Tours

History of the Franks

IV, 28 and V, 39

Seeing that his half-brother Sigibert had made a good marriage, King Chilperic was ashamed of being linked only with women of inferior rank. Even though he already had several wives, he sent envoys to ask for Galswintha, the sister of Sigibert's wife Brunhilda, promising through these envoys that he would leave all the others when he had acquired a consort – a king's daughter – worthy of himself. Galswintha's father, King Athanagild of the Visigoths, accepted his promises and sent him his daughter, with a large amount of riches as a dowry, as he had done for his other daughter. When she arrived, Galswintha was received with great honour and was married to Chilperic, who treated her with all the more affection because of the great amount of treasure she had brought with her.

But soon his love for Fredegonda, whom he had earlier taken as a concubine, was to cause a great problem. Galswintha had already adopted the Catholic faith and had been baptised, and now she complained daily to the king of being insulted, declaring that no-one showed her any respect; she demanded to be returned to her own country, leaving behind the treasures she had brought with her. First of all Chilperic tried subterfuge, calming her down and speaking sweetly to her, but eventually he had her strangled by one of his men, so that she was discovered dead in her bed. Chilperic pretended to mourn her death, but after a few days he married Fredegonda. His brothers, who reckoned that it was at the instigation of this woman that Galswintha had perished, forced him (temporarily) from the throne. Chilperic had three sons by one of his earlier wives, named Audovera. These were Theodebert, Merovech and Clovis . . .

After the death of their own sons, Chilperic and Fredegonda,

45

bowed down with grief, retired to spend the month of October in the fortress situated in the middle of the forest of Villers-Cotterets. Fredegonda persuaded her husband to send his son, Clovis, to Berny; she was hoping that he would fall victim to the sickness which had already caused the death of his half-brothers and which was still raging there as a violent epidemic. But it spared Clovis, and he was not bothered by it at all.

The king went back to Chelles, an estate near Paris, and a few days after arriving at his residence there, sent for Clovis to come to him.

And now I shall tell you how the young prince met his end. While he was at Chelles with his father, he had some imprudent conversations and said some rather unwise things, to the effect that now that his brothers were dead he was assured of the throne, and that all Gaul would be his, and that his empire would be limitless – that at last his enemies would fall into his hands and that he could do with them what he liked. He also made comments and serious accusations about his step-mother Fredegonda. The queen heard of this, was worried, and determined to take steps to prevent any difficulties for herself.

A few days later, someone came to the queen (probably well-coached in the role) and said: 'O queen, if you have lost your children, the blame for this is Clovis' alone! He is in love with one of your ladies-in-waiting, whose mother is an adept in magic, and she caused the death of your sons by sorcery. I am giving you this information as a warning to yourself, because you can't hope for any better fate yourself than that met by your children.'

Then Fredegonda, pretending to be terrified by this, but really in a complete rage, had her men seize the girl that Clovis had been casting his eyes over, had her stripped and thrashed with canes, then had her long and beautiful hair cut off and fixed to a stake outside Clovis' lodging. The girl's mother was arrested, imprisoned and tortured so violently that she confessed that the charges against her were true.

Fredegonda hurried to Chilperic, and by a mixture of pleading and demanding, cajoling and shouting, she obtained the right of revenge on Clovis. The king was going hunting, and sent word to Clovis to join him. When the prince arrived, two of the king's dukes, Didier and Bobon, acting on orders, grabbed him and disarmed him. He was stripped of his fine clothes and given coarse ones, put in chains and handed over to the queen.

The queen kept him in jail for three days, trying to see if she could not get out of him some kind of confession that would damn him. But the prince denied everything with great indignation, although he did name a great number of his close associates.

After three days, Fredegonda had him manacled and transported down the Marne to an estate at Nogent. He was to be well guarded there, and while he was imprisoned a knife was plunged into his heart and he was buried in the cell in which he had been kept. Meanwhile, messengers were sent to the king to announce that Clovis had committed suicide by stabbing himself, adding as confirmation that the knife was still in his chest. Taken in by this report, the king did not shed a single tear for the one he had delivered up to his death at the instigation of the queen. All those who had been attached to Clovis were now hunted out wherever they were. His mother, Audovera, at this time a nun in Le Mans, was snatched from her convent and murdered while begging for mercy. His sister, Childerinda, was taken to a convent by Fredegonda's servants, and made to change her clothes, after which she was locked in and remains there to this day. All the property of Audovera and her daughter were confiscated for the use of Queen Fredegonda.

The woman who had confessed against Clovis under torture, was now condemned to be burned. The unfortunate woman protested her innocence and that of Clovis, saying that the supposed confession was a pack of lies. But she protested in vain: she was tied to a stake and burned alive.

Charlemagne

The Roman Empire was officially reconstituted (in theory, anyway) by a later Frankish king, Charles, known as 'the Great,' a man of whom even Gibbon approved, raising his eyebrows only at his vigorous sex-life. His biographer (and friend) Einhard mentions several wives and concubines (a man of some stamina, Charlemagne once had four at the same time), and Einhard occasionally remembers others as he writes. His picture of Charlemagne's private life is revealing, especially when compared with that of the Roman emperors in Suetonius' *Twelve Caesars*, which Einhard is imitating. Note those baths, again. Einhard wrote his Latin biography between 829 and 836.

Einhard

The Life of Charlemagne

XXII–XXV

Charlemagne was strong and tough in his body, and also tall (though not excessively – his height was the equivalent of seven times the measure of one of his feet). His head was rounded at the top, and his eyes were large and bright. His nose was slightly longer than the average and he had white hair, which suited him. His face was open and good-natured. Whether standing or sitting, he always had an air of authority and dignity because of these things. His neck was rather short and thick, and he had something of a pot-belly, but the rest of his body balanced out these features. His movements were all firm and manly. His voice was loud, but less so than you would expect from his size. He enjoyed good health, except for the last four years of his life when he often had fevers, and, at the end, he was lame in one foot. Even then he used to do what he wanted, whatever the doctors said, and he came to dislike them anyway, because they advised him to give up the roast meat which he was used to, and eat stewed food instead.

He exercised a great deal, riding or hunting, and there is hardly another nation on earth that can match the Franks in this. He took great delight in steam-baths at thermal springs, and he often used to swim, a sport in which no-one could beat him. For this reason it was at Aachen that he built his palace, and he stayed there right up to the end of his life. He used to invite not only his sons to bathe with him, but also his noblemen and his friends, and sometimes even a whole mob of attendants and bodyguards, so that sometimes a hundred men or more would be taking a bath together.

He wore national costume – of the Franks, that is. Next to his skin he wore a linen undershirt and underpants, then a tunic edged with silk, and then hose. On his feet he wore shoes and foot-cloths, and in the winter protected his chest

49

and shoulders with an otterskin or ermine jacket. He wore a blue military cloak and always carried a sword at his side, with a gold or silver hilt and belt. Sometimes he would use a jewelled sword, but this was reserved for great feasts, or when legates from abroad were present. He disliked other national costumes, however fine, and would never wear them, except once in Rome, at the request of Pope Hadrian, and then again when asked by Hadrian's sucessor, Leo, he put on a long tunic and a cloak in the Greek style, and Roman shoes. On feast-days he would appear dressed in cloth-of-gold, with jewelled shoes, a golden brooch pinning his cloak, and a diadem of gold and gems on his head. On other days, his clothes were hardly different from those of ordinary people.

He was not excessive in his eating and drinking habits, especially the latter, because he abominated drunkenness in any one, especially his friends or himself. However, he could not go for long times without food, and often said that fasting made him physically ill. He rarely held a large-scale feast, and then only on the major festivals; however, there would then be a very large number of men invited. His dinner on ordinary days consisted of four courses, quite apart from the roast, which his hunters brought in on a spit, and which was his favourite food . . .

He learned Latin grammar from the elderly Peter the Deacon, of Pisa, and for other disciplines his teacher was Alcuin Albinus, also a Deacon, a Saxon from Britain, and the most learned man anywhere. From him Charlemagne learned rhetoric and dialectic, and especially astrology, and devoted much time and effort to this. He studied computation, and with interest and care traced the courses of the stars. He also tried to learn to write, and used to keep writing-tablets and little notebooks under the pillows on his bed, so that he could practise forming letters in his spare time. However, although he tried hard, he had really come to it too late.

THE RULING CLASSES

Medieval history provides plenty of examples of misdeeds, chaos and political decay, as well as what nowadays would just be good tabloid newspaper copy. Members of the ruling class have always been capable of behaving badly, and sometimes they came to a spectacularly sticky end. Even royalty could prove to be degenerate. As far as the aristocracy goes, the most notorious noble of the Middle Ages was Gilles de Rais, who was associated in his earlier years with Joan of Arc, but who latterly came rather closer to the gargoyles than the saints. Nevertheless, he died penitent.

Charlemagne's Grandchildren

One of the dottier Frankish customs was the division of property and land between *all* legitimate male heirs, a system which led inevitably either to murder or to complex inter-necine alliances and treaties. Charlemagne had left only one heir to his lands, but when *he* died, the empire really fell apart. After a very important battle (which is rarely mentioned in British textbooks), Europe was left with concepts like 'France,' 'Germany' and, even more unfortunately, 'Alsace-Lorraine,' a source of confusion ever since. These extracts from a Latin contemporary report show two of his grandsons, Charles and Ludwig, kings of what became France and Germany, ganging up on the third, Lothar, who was the eldest, and hence (nominally) emperor. A fourth brother, Pepin the Elder, was already dead. The writer of the chronicle, Nithard was one of two illegitimate sons of abbot Angilbert of St-Riquier, born to Charlemagne's daughter Bertha while Angilbert (a notable poet) was at Charle-magne's court. The other was called, with a certain lack of imagination, Hartnid. Angilbert was a lay abbot of the monastery, but Nithard reports in the same chronicle how, twenty-seven years after his death, his tomb fell open in an earth-quake and the body was found to be uncorrupted, a sure sign of sainthood, whatever his intramural activities at Charle-magne's court had been. Nithard also wanted to be lay abbot of St-Riquier (contesting this plum appointment with an-other more clerical grandson of Charlemagne), but was killed not long after he finished (or rather, somewhat huffily gave up writing) his chronicle. He was commissioned to write the report by King Charles (later 'the Bald'), to whose retinue he belonged.

Nithard

Histories

II, 10–III, 5 (for the year 841)

At daybreak Ludwig and Charles sent envoys to Lothar, and
had them say to him that it was very painful to them that he
had refused peace and demanded battle. Since he wanted it,
though, and if there was no alternative, then so be it, but it
must be done fairly. First of all they should fast and pray to
God, and then they promised Lothar to let him come across
to them and give him an opportunity to meet them in open
battle without any deceit or cheating, after all obstacles had
been removed from both sides. If he agreed to this, the
envoys should declare this under oath. If not, then they asked
him to agree the same terms for them, and declare that under
oath. However, Lothar followed his usual custom and said
that he would answer via his own envoys; but as soon as their
envoys had left, Lothar set out to meet his ally, his nephew
King Pepin the Younger of Aquitaine, and headed for
Fontenoy-en-Puisaye to set up camp. However, his two brothers – hurrying after Lothar – set out on the same day, over-
took him and set up their camp by a place called Thury. The
next day both armies, ready for battle, moved a little way out
of their camps, but first of all Ludwig and Charles sent
envoys to Lothar asking him to think of his role as their
brother, and to grant peace to God's church and the Christian people by not taking away from the lands left to them by
their father – with his agreement. They added that he could
keep the land which their father had left to him, though he
had done so only out of kindness, and not because Lothar
deserved it. Furthermore they offered him as a gift everything of value in their camp (except horses and weapons).
And if he did not agree to this, they would each give him a
portion of their own lands. Failing that, the Frankish territo-
ries should be divided into equal parts, and he could choose
to rule whichever he wanted. As usual, Lothar answered that

he would send his own envoys with his decision, and this time he really did send Drogo, Hugo and Hegibert, who said that these proposals were new ones, and that therefore he needed time to consider them. In fact, however, Pepin had not yet arrived, and he wanted to use the delay to wait for him. Nevertheless, he did have their envoys Ricuin, Hirmenald and Friedrich assured under oath that nothing else prompted him to ask for this stay of battle but the desire to further the common good, both for his brothers and for the people as a whole, which is what justice between brothers and Christians demanded. Charles and Ludwig believed his oath, and returned to their camp, after an armistice had been sworn for this and the following day, and on to the second daylight hour of the third day, June 25. The next day they wanted to celebrate the feast of St John the Baptist, but by now Pepin had turned up to assist Lothar, who sent word to his brothers that they were well aware that the imperial title had been given to him in all solemnity, and that they should think about how he was to fulfil the heavy and important demands of this high office. He was, of course, still mindful of mutual benefits. However, when the envoys were asked whether Lothar was inclined to accept any of the proposals put to him, or whether he had empowered them to give a definite decision, they answered that they had been told nothing of that sort. With this, any hopes of justice and peace from Lothar seemed to vanish, so they sent word to him that if he could not come up with a better solution, then he should either agree to one of their proposals or understand that at the second hour of the next day – June 25 – they would come for him, to submit the matter to the judgement of Almighty God, something which he had forced them to do. In his usual manner, Lothar arrogantly rejected this, and replied that they would see later what he decided. (By the way, while I was writing this down – on October 18, 841 – at St Cloud on the Loire, there was an eclipse of the sun in Scorpio in the first daylight hour.) After this breakdown of negotiations, Charles and Ludwig set out with their armies at dawn, and with about a third of their troops occupied a hill near Lothar's camp, where they waited for his arrival at the second daylight hour, according to the arrangement. And when both sides were there they joined in a fierce battle by the stream. Ludwig and Lothar met in violent combat at the place called Brittas, and Lothar was beaten off and fled. The part of Lothar's forces that Charles faced, at a place called Fagit, also fled; that part, however, which had attacked our man Adelhard and the rest at Solennat – where I myself, with God's help, gave no small amount of assistance – fought hard, so that the battle went on for a long time. However, eventually all of Lothar's men fled the field . . .

Lothar reached Sens, which is what he had arranged with Pepin, but was uncertain as to what to do next, because Charles had sent part of his army across the Seine, then into and through a wood known locally as La Perche. Lothar was afraid that this could prove an obstacle for him or his allies, and so he decided on a pre-emptive strike, in the hope of wiping them out quickly, and bringing the rest down because of the shock. He was especially concerned to bring to heel the Breton Duke Nomenoi. But all his plans were in vain and he was unable to do any of this, because Charles' army got away from him untouched, he gained no followers, and Duke Nomenoi ignored pointedly all of Lothar's commands. In this condition, Lothar suddenly received the news that Ludwig and Charles were preparing a great army together. Seeing himself surrounded with difficulties on all sides he first made a great and unnecessary detour, then retreated from Tours and eventually reached his lands with an exhausted army. Pepin the Younger, who was regretting having joined forces with Lothar, returned to Aquitaine. Meanwhile Charles heard that Bishop Otgar of Mainz and others were preventing his brother Ludwig from crossing the Rhine, and moved quickly via Toul into Alsace. When Otgar heard of this, he and his supporters quickly left the Rhine and escaped wherever they could.

And so, on February 14, Ludwig and Charles arrived in Strasbourg, and swore the following oath of mutual non-aggression, Ludwig doing so in French and Charles in

German. And before they did so, they addressed their respective armies in their own languages, Ludwig speaking in German, Charles in French. Ludwig, as the elder brother, spoke first, and said: 'You all know how often Lothar, since the death of our father, has attacked me and my brother and has tried to destroy us utterly; since neither brotherly love, nor Christian morality, nor any appeals to reason proved the slightest use to make for a just peace between us, we were eventually forced by circumstances to leave the judgement to God, and agreed to accept whatever decision He made. As you know, we emerged victorious from the battle through God's grace; Lothar was conquered and fled with his men as far away as he could. Now, through fraternal love and through mercy for his Christian people we did not follow them nor did we destroy them, but we have demanded, as we did before, that he should give us our rights. Instead of accepting God's judgement, however, Lothar has not ceased to pursue me and my brother with force of arms as an enemy, and to destroy our people with fire, plundering and murder. Therefore we are compelled to join forces, and in case you had any doubts about our good faith and undying brotherly love, we have decided to swear this oath between us before your eyes. We are not doing this out of any unjust desires, but to provide – if God grants us peace with your help – a treaty that will be for the common good. And in the unlikely event of my breaking the oath which I am about to swear towards my brother, then this would make you free from the oath that you have sworn to me.' And after Charles had said the same words to his men in French, Ludwig, again as the elder, swore the actual oath first: 'For the love of God and for the Christian people, and for our salvation from this day on-wards, so long as God grants me strength, I shall support my brother Charles in all things, as one should as a brother, provided he does the same for me. And I shall enter into no agreements with Lothar that as far as I can see might hurt my brother Charles.' And when Ludwig had finished, Charles swore the same oath in German for Ludwig's army.

Having too firm a ruler can be a problem; having a weak one is probably worse. Although there is not even a mention of the counter-claim to the throne by the Empress Matilda (who only seems to get a mention these days in novels by Ellis Peters), it is clear from this very famous extract from the *Anglo-Saxon Chronicle* on the breakdown of law and order that Stephen was never really up to the job of being a medieval king.

The Peterborough Chronicle

In 1137 King Stephen went across to Normandy and was well received there, because people thought that he would be just like his uncle, Henry I, and also because he still held the royal treasury. However, he gave it away or spent it foolishly. King Henry had accumulated a great deal of gold and silver, but it was not used for the good of his soul.

When King Stephen returned to England he called a council at Oxford, and arrested Roger, Bishop of Salisbury, and also Alexander, Bishop of Lincoln and Roger the Chancellor, his nephews, putting them in prison until they surrendered their castles to him. But when the traitors in the land saw that Stephen was of a mild disposition, soft and kind-hearted, and unable to impose justice, they committed all kinds of atrocities. They had declared their loyalty to him and had sworn oaths, but reneged on all of this. All the oaths were false and they were all broken, because every rich man built a castle and held it against the king – the whole country was full of these castles, and the poor people of the land were greatly overworked in building them. When the castles had all been built, they filled them with veritable devils and wicked men. Both by night and by day they would seize men (and women) that they thought had any property, and put them into prison for the sake of their gold and silver, and tortured them in unspeakable fashion – the holy martyrs were never subjected to such pain as this. Some were hung up by the feet and suffocated with foul smoke. Some were hung up by the thumbs, others by the head, and they had heavy chain-mail coats tied to their feet. Some had knotted cords tied around their heads, which were then twisted so that the knots penetrated the brain. Some were placed into dungeons with vipers and other snakes and toads, and were killed that way. Others again were placed inside an instrument of torture made like a short, narrow and shallow box, and sharp stones were put in it so that the man inside was crushed and all the bones in his body broken. The torture-chambers of many of these castles had a special instrument consisting of a head-band and halter, which was so heavy that it took two or three men to carry one. It was constructed as follows: it was fastened to a beam and a sharp metal halter was put round a man's throat and neck in such a way that he could move in no direction, not sit, lie or sleep, because of the weight of all that iron. Many thousands died of starvation. I cannot and will not tell of all the atrocities and all the tortures that were perpetrated upon this land, and which went on for the nineteen years that Stephen was king, getting worse and worse. Every so often they would impose a tax on the towns, which they called 'insurance money.' When the wretched people had no more to give, they plundered and burned the settlements, so that it was easy to travel for a whole day and not find a settlement that wasn't deserted, or land that had been tilled. Corn was dear, and so was meat, cheese and butter, because there was none to be had in the land. Many poor wretches died of starvation, while others, who had once been wealthy, were forced to beg in the streets. Others fled the country. There was never a land more wretched, nor did heathen men ever behave as badly, for in all their wantonness they spared neither church nor churchyard, but stole everything there was to steal, and then set fire to the church and all its buildings. Nor, indeed, did they spare the lands of bishops, abbots or priests, but they plundered monks and clergymen, and everyone robbed his neighbour. If two or three men ever rode together towards a

58

town, all the inhabitants would flee, because they assumed that these were robbers. Bishops and clergy pronounced curses upon them, but it made no difference to them, since they were all excommunicated, damned and lost. When the land was actually tilled, the corn would not grow because the earth was ruined. It was said openly that 'Christ and His saints were sleeping.' We had to suffer things like this – and more than we can tell – for nineteen years, for our sins.

Richard I

The reign of Richard I (1189-99) is interesting partly because the old super-hero image of the Lionheart is now a little tarnished. He wasn't the best king for England; he rarely visited it, preferring Aquitaine, Sicily, wars in the middle east, and some not very competent political wheeling-and-dealing with the French, the Austrians and others. Three short extracts from Latin histories make the point, one from the huge *Polychronicon* of Ranulph Higden (d. 1364), a Benedictine from Chester, one from the *History of England* by the Yorkshire monk William of Newburgh (d. 1198), and one from the *Minor Chronicle* of Matthew Paris (d. 1259), the historian-monk of St Albans. The first shows Richard's unpleasant Lord Chancellor, William Longchamp, Bishop of Ely, singularly failing to disguise himself as a woman; the second documents an even darker side of the Crusaders as they robbed Jewish communities in England (with additional problems that had to be sorted out by St Hugh); the third shows how Richard was bailed out, as usual, by the English taxpayer.

Ranulph Higden

The Polychronicon

VII

The notoriety of the wicked Lord Chancellor, William Long-champ, filled all England, so that great men complained and lesser men cursed him. John, the King's brother, was extremely angry because William had taken prisoner their half-brother, Geoffrey the Bastard, Archbishop-elect of York, so he gathered together a large number of troops from his own lands and from Wales, and pursued the common tyrant from Windsor to the Tower of London, and then further on, to Dover. When he got there, William was much afraid that he would not be able to cross the Channel freely, so he put on women's clothing over his ecclesiastical vestments, covering his head and much of his face with a kerchief. He walked along the shore with a length of linen over his left arm as if he were selling it, and carried a yardstick in the other, thinking that by this trick he would not be spotted and could escape more easily. But because he was quite unable to open or close his garments like a woman, he was caught – quite literally – by the private parts, and thus exposed in a most ignominious fashion. However, he eventually got away, and the administration of the kingdom passed to the Bishop of Rouen.

William of Newburgh

History of England

IV, 8

After the massacre of the Jews at King's Lynn there was a new rising against the Jews in Stamford. There, at a market-fair at the beginning of Lent a crowd of young men from various places, who had assembled to take the Cross of Our Lord before setting out for Jerusalem, were indignant that the enemies of Christ's Cross who lived there should possess so much wealth when they themselves had so much less to go on their journey with; and so they took by force from the supposedly undeserving owners of this wealth what they needed for their forthcoming pilgrimage. Reckoning that they were doing service to Christ by attacking His enemies (whose property they were after), they boldly set upon them, and no-one, whether native to the place or whether they had come in for the fair, dared to resist so many. Several of the Jews were killed, while others escaped wounded to the Castle. Their homes were looted and a great deal of money stolen. The robbers got away with the booty from their deeds, and none gave any thought to public order. One of them, a cocky young man from Northampton, whose name was John, left his share of the money with someone, and was secretly murdered by him for the sake of that cash. His body was thrown out of the town at night, but was found and by chance was recognised by someone, and the greedy killer fled. Soon, there were reports of dreams, visions and supernatural magic at that place, and simple folk attributed to the dead man all the merit and glory of a martyr, and they kept solemn vigils over his burial-place. The fame of the dead man spread amongst the ordinary people, who came there in curiosity and devotion, first from the immediate area and then later from further afield; and no-one who came to the new martyr, either to see the miracles or to seek aid, came empty-handed. This was mocked by the wise, but welcomed by the clerics who did well out of this superstition. The matter was referred to Bishop Hugh of Lincoln, a man of the greatest virtue, who boldly visited the place and removed all the trappings of the false martyr, and by Papal authority and under pain of excommunication he put a stop to the superstitious veneration of this dead man. Thus, by the pious and effective intervention of this saintly pastor, the affair was brought to an end and the nonsense stopped.

Matthew Paris

The History of the English (The Minor Chronicle)

HOW THE DUKE OF AUSTRIA SOLD KING RICHARD TO THE EMPEROR

In the year of grace 1193 King Richard was in the custody of Leopold, Duke of Austria, who then sold him to the Holy Roman Emperor, Henry VI, for sixty thousand pounds of silver (reckoned on the Cologne standard). And when he had taken him, the Emperor kept him very well guarded indeed. In order to hold the King so as to exchange him for an enormous cash ransom, he had him imprisoned at Trifels, from which prison no-one had thus far ever escaped, and in which it was reckoned to be crueller to lock a man up than to kill him — the place was notorious. There he was kept prisoner under the guard of a large number of armed soldiers with swords at the ready. All this was quite unable to put the most noble Richard out of countenance, and he seems always to have laughed and joked or acted in a bold manner, according as time, place, circumstances or people dictated. So as not to delay the course of this history, however, I shall leave others to relate these amazing things about him.

HOW THE EMPEROR ACCUSED RICHARD OF A VARIETY OF SERIOUS CRIMES

The Emperor had been extremely angry with and greatly inimical towards the King for a long time, and would on no account allow him to plead before him, because he wanted to make a serious accusation of a number of crimes. Eventually, after the intervention of his friends, notably the Abbot of Cluny and William Longchamp, Richard's Chancellor, the Emperor ordered the King to be brought into his presence with all solemnity, having summoned all his bishops, dukes and counts, and accused him directly in public of a variety of crimes . . . However, when King Richard was charged by the Emperor with all these calumnies, he stood right in the open, and although he had been called murderous, arrogant and villainous, he spoke so splendidly and rhetorically against each of the charges, that he drew the admiration of all, so much so that no suspicion of guilt for any of the things of which he had been accused remained in the minds of any of those listening. And so, when he had put his case for a long time before the Emperor and his princes, justifying himself so persuasively, the Emperor, much admiring this great eloquence on the King's part, and also his steadfastness in the face of his tribulations, stood up and drew the King towards him to embrace him. From that day onward the Emperor began to deal with Richard more kindly, and to treat him with honour.

HOW KING RICHARD RAISED ONE HUNDRED AND FORTY THOUSAND POUNDS OF SILVER FOR HIS RANSOM

After all this, and with his friends again acting as mediators, there were long discussions about the King's ransom. Eventually it was agreed that in exchange for Richard's release the Emperor should be given one hundred and forty thousand marks of Cologne-standard silver, all of which would have to be found before he was freed. Thus an oath was taken on June 29, the feast of Saints Peter and Paul, by the bishops, dukes and barons, that the King should be enabled to raise that sum as soon as possible, so that he could return home. The substance of this agreement was conveyed back to England by Lord Chancellor William, Bishop of Ely, who took with him the King's letters with the golden seal of the Emperor upon them, and right away he issued an edict by the King's justices that all bishops, clerics, earls and barons, abbots and priors should give up one quarter of their income for the release of the King. Over and above this the Church contributed its chalices and the Cistercian Order a year's wool-tax. No church and no monastic order was exempt.

John, Bishop of Norwich, indeed, gathered half of the value of the chalices in his whole diocese to this end, and added half of his own fortune. So too, Abbot Warin of St Albans added a hundred marks of silver of his own to that of his diocese and church. Hugh, Bishop of Chester, who had with great assiduousness gathered many great gifts for the King's cause was, when staying near Canterbury, robbed during the night of everything he had. However, Matthew de Clere, Constable of Dover, had aided and abetted the thieves, and for that the Archbishop of Canterbury excommunicated him.

Edward II

Edward II or Edward of Caernarvon (1307-1327) is another of the more confusing English monarchs. His sexual orientation has been discussed, and his less than half-hearted Scottish campaign led to Bannockburn in 1314. But he remains known primarily for his habit of allowing the kingdom to be run by ill-chosen favourites like Piers Gaveston, actually of a good Gascon family, but widely viewed in England as a grubby upstart and killed in 1312, or Hugh Despenser (ditto, in 1326). Edward himself was murdered in 1327, the prime movers being his wife Isabella, unaffectionately known as the 'She-Wolf of France,' and her lover, Mortimer. Isabella was tough where Edward was weak (rather than wicked, and he *was* fit and strong physically, which made him difficult to kill); but their son ruled as Edward III for nearly fifty years. The extracts are from three Latin chronicles: the anonymous London *Annals of St Paul's* (on the general unpopularity of Piers Gaveston); the *History of England 1272–1381* by Thomas of Walsingham, another monk of St Albans (on the necessarily very visible public death of Despenser); and Sir Thomas de la Moore's account in his *Life and Death of Edward II*, composed about twenty years after the events, of the dreadful end of Edward himself, which, unlike that of Hugh, had to *look* as if it had been natural, even if his screams had been heard for miles around.

The Annals of St Paul's

1308

In that year King Edward kept Christmas with Piers Gaveston at Wye, in a manor belonging to Battle Abbey. It was at this time that the Pope, seeking peace between the two kingdoms of France and England, confirmed the marriage which King Edward I had, in his wisdom, arranged long before, joining in matrimony the daughter of King Philip of France, that is, and Edward, son of King Edward I of England. Having made preparations for the marriage, the king gave the custody of the kingdom into the hands of Gaveston, and set out on January 22 for Boulogne, where he was received by the King of France with delight and great honour, for Philip had been eagerly awaiting him for some time. And so the King of England married Isabella, daughter of the King of France, at St Mary's in Boulogne, on January 25, 1308. At the festivities were dukes and earls from thirty-two different countries, not counting those who had come across the sea with Edward. The King of France gave his new son-in-law, the King of England, the seal-ring of his kingdom, a marriage-bed more beautiful than had ever been seen, some superb war-horses, and many other gifts, gifts without number. All these the King of England sent right away to Piers Gaveston. Then, after several days of wedding-feasts, and after he had done homage to the King of France for the lands he held from him, King Edward returned on February 7, with his wife Isabella, to England.

But Piers Gaveston, named Earl of Cornwall, though a complete upstart, now began to despise the English. He had organised a tournament in honour of his own wife at Wallingford, with sixty knights entered against the same number. But on the appointed day he cheated by entering the field with two hundred armed warriors, and put to flight any of them that got in his way. From this arose much indignation on the part of the English. On another day a second tournament was proclaimed between two sides at Faversham in Kent, in celebration of the King's wedding. This time on the appointed day he craftily feigned fighting, openly mocking the barons. This led to even greater annoyance on the part of the earls and nobles. A third tournament was proclaimed, in honour of the King's coronation, at Stepney. Gaveston was afraid to go there, and suggested to the King that the nobles were planning to kill him, and the King at once forbade the tournament. Everywhere one could hear murmurings against Gaveston, and words of hatred from the people. But however great the hatred on the part of worthy men became against this man – who had been raised from the dungheap – the more fervent in proportion to it grew the love of the King for Piers Gaveston. Because of his excessive affection for him, the King referred to Gaveston as his 'brother.' But the world at large used to call him the King's 'idol,' whom the king was as afraid to annoy as if Piers had been his father, and as eager to please as if he had been his superior. The King had in his gift various kinds of favour, which were his to dispense by his own royal prerogative – they were his own, and it was inappropriate for them to be in the hands of anyone else, but he transferred their operation to Gaveston. Now, if one of the nobles or lords required a special favour of the King in some matter that needed settlement, the King sent him to Piers Gaveston, and whatever he ordered or said, that would soon be done, and the King accepted this. But the whole population was angry about the situation of having two kings ruling the land, one in name and one in reality.

Thomas of Walsingham

A History of England

1326

After this, the aforementioned Sir Hugh Despenser [the Younger] was condemned to death without right of appeal at Hereford, and was there dragged through the streets, then hanged on a gallows that was fifty feet high. Then he was decapitated and quartered, and the four pieces sent to the four parts of the kingdom. His head, though, was placed on London Bridge. He had been dragged through the street in a surcote with his own arms on it, on which was clearly written in fine letters the words of Psalm LII, from 'Why boasteth thou thyself in mischief' down to 'I am like the green olive tree.' And afterwards it was written of him:

The rope, the wood, the sword, the flame did take from you,
with axe and horse, your great pride at the last, Sir Hugh.

A rope, because of the dragging; wood, because he was hanged; the sword, because he was beheaded; flame, because he was disembowelled and his intestines were burned; an axe, because he was chopped into quarters; and a horse, again because he was dragged through the streets.

On the same day, Simon de Reading was also dragged through the streets and hanged on the same gallows as was used for Hugh, but ten feet lower.

Sir Thomas de la Moore

The Life and Death of Edward II

Now began the arrangements for the final persecution of Edward, a persecution to the death. First of all he was locked securely in a chamber in which, over a period of many days, he was nearly brought to suffocation from the stench of corpses in the room beneath; the intolerable stink from that place was the greatest suffering he had ever borne, and one day Edward, the servant of God, complained from a window to carpenters who were working there. His oppressors saw that death could not conquer such a strong man just by a stench, and on the night of September 21, when he was in bed, he was suddenly taken by surprise and held down and suffocated with bolsters and with the weight of more than fifteen strong men; then, with an iron rod which had been heated until it was red-hot, they burned his intestines by passing it down a tube into his insides through his back passage, taking care that no wounds were visible on the royal body in places where one might look for wounds – for if manifest wounds were found by some friends of justice, his murderers might be made to submit themselves for punishment. And so the strong warrior was overcome, and emitted cries that could be heard inside and outside Berkeley Castle, enough to make known the extent of the violence at the death of the victim. Indeed, the cries of the dying man led many in Berkeley, including some of the castle guards (as they themselves said) to compassion and prayer for the immortal soul of the dying man. Thus can the world turn its hatred upon a man, just as it did before to his master, Jesus Christ; the leader was shunned by the kingdom of the Jews, while His disciple was robbed of the kingdom of England, but received into the heights of the angelic kingdom.

Persecution by Isabella and by the Bishop of Hereford (so that it might look as if *they* had clean hands and pure hearts) outlawed and drove into exile the perpetrators, Thomas de Gournay and Sir John Maltravers. Three years later Gournay, hiding out as a fugitive in Marseilles, was recognised, captured and brought back to England to receive his punishment, and was beheaded at sea, for fear that he might accuse the nobles and great prelates and others in the kingdom of involvement in his crime, and of having given their assent. The other one, however, Maltravers, remained in hiding for a long time in Germany.

Pedro the Cruel

Medieval kings attracted some interesting soubriquets; the Carolingians produced Lewis the Pious, Charles the Bald, Charles the Fat and others. But a king probably had to make a real effort to get the title 'the Cruel,' and King Peter or Pedro IV of Castile (1334–69) seems to have merited it more than many others (although 'Vlad the Impaler' is another name to conjure with). H. J. Chaytor said in 1929 that Pedro's character 'can be most charitably summarized as the outcome of homicidal mania.' Pedro's story is also surprisingly modern in that his regime was propped up by foreign governments, England amongst them, at least for a while. The great French history by Jean Froissart (1337–1410), from which these extracts are taken, was translated into English by John Bourchier, Lord Berners (1467–1533), although his text now needs translating, even if it has its high moments, as when Pedro's half-brothers are 'right sore displeased and good cause why', after he had slaughtered their mother. Incidentally, 'Bastard' in this context is entirely technical and without opprobrium.

Jean Froissart

The Chronicles

I, 229f.

At that time there was a King in Castile called Don Pedro, a man full of arrogant opinions, crude and rebellious against the commandments of Holy Church. He wanted to subdue all neighbouring Christian kings and princes, especially Pedro IV of Aragon, a good, true Christian prince, and had taken from him part of his realm, with a view to taking the rest of it as well. Furthermore, Pedro of Castile had three illegitimate brothers, which his father, King Alfonso XI, had had by a lady called Eleanor de Guzman, known as *la richa Doña*. The eldest was called Henry, the second Don Tello, and the third Sancho. King Pedro hated them and would not allow them in his sight, and many a time he would have struck off their heads if he had been able to capture them. But they had been loved by King Alfonso, their father, and in his life he gave Henry, the eldest, the county of Astorga, but King Pedro, his half-brother, had taken it from him, and therefore they were permanently at war with each other. Henry the Bastard, however, was a very brave and valiant knight, and had been at war in France for a long time, and had served the French king, who loved him dearly. It was rumoured widely that King Pedro had put to death the mother of the three brothers, and they were rightly very angry about this. Beside that, he had put to death or exiled various great lords of the realm of Castile, and was so cruel and without shame that all his men feared, distrusted and hated him as far as possible. Also he had caused the death of the good and holy lady to whom he was married, namely the Lady Blanche, daughter of Pierre, Duke of Bourbon, cousin to the French Queen and to the Countess of Savoy; this death much angered her family, which was one of the noblest families in the world. Furthermore, it was also rumoured amongst his own men that he had made an alliance with the Emir of Granada, the

Marinid Sultan and the Emir of Tlemçen, all of whom were God's enemies and unbelievers. Because of this, some of his own men were afraid that he would cause damage to his own country by violating God's churches, for he was already beginning to misappropriate their rents and revenues and to keep some of the prelates in prison in a tyrannous fashion, on account of which daily complaints were made to our Holy Father the Pope, asking him to find some remedy for all this. The Pope agreed readily to these requests, and swiftly sent messengers into Castile to King Pedro, commanding him to come in person at once to Rome without delay, to cleanse and purge himself of such villainous deeds as he was guilty of. However, King Pedro was full of pride and presumptuousness, and would neither obey nor come there, but dealt shamefully with the papal messengers, which incurred the wrath of the Church and of our Holy Father the Pope. Thus this evil King Pedro persevered still in his obstinacy. Therefore, the Pope and the Curia took counsel as to how they might correct him, and there it was decided that he was not worthy of the name of king, nor should he hold any kingdom. And in full consistory in Avignon, in the chamber of excommunication, he was openly declared to be reputed to be an unbeliever. It was considered that he should be constrained and corrected by a group of companions then in the realm of France. Then the King of Aragon, who hated the King of Castile, was sent for, and also Henry the Bastard of Spain, that they should come to the Pope at Avignon. And when they arrived, the Pope made Henry, Bastard of Spain, legitimate and lawful ruler of the realm of Castile, and Pedro was cursed and condemned by sentence of the Pope . . .

As I have shown before, this King Pedro was much hated by his own men throughout all the realm of Castile because of his incredibly cruel acts of punishment and for his destruction of noble men in his kingdom, men whom he put to death and slew with his own hands. Because of this, as soon as they saw his brother Henry enter the realm with a great force, they rallied to him and received him as their lord, and rode out with him, and caused cities, towns, boroughs and castles to be opened to him, and everyone did homage to him. And so the Spaniards cried with one voice: 'Long live Henry! Death to Pedro!' [. . .]

Gilles de Rais

Gilles de Rais was born in 1404, became a Marshal of France, and assisted Joan of Arc against the English. St Joan was executed in 1431 (although Gilles was associated in 1439 with a false Joan, who claimed to have escaped the flames). Gilles is best known, however, for his abuse and murder of a large number of children in the 1430s. Records of the trial of what we would now call a serial killer make thoroughly unpleasant reading, and only extracts bear translation. Most of it cannot and should not be read for entertainment of any kind, so concentration here is on the details of his inept and apparently not very successful attempts to invoke demons, rather than his murders of children and his unnatural vices. He was tried for religious and secular crimes, confessed, and declared himself penitent. The real number of his victims is unknown – around two hundred? He was hanged, but his body was saved from being burned, and he was buried (by several noble ladies) in Nantes. He lives on as one of the prototypes for the Bluebeard story, although devil-worship and child-abuse are not really part of that legend, even if murder is.

Documents of the Trials of Gilles de Rais

Confession of Gilles de Rais

Saturday, October 22, 1440

The aforesaid Gilles de Rais, the accused, confessed voluntarily and in public that he, for his own private delectation, had taken or arranged to have taken such a large number of children that he no longer knew the precise number, and that he killed them or had them killed, and had committed upon them the sin and vice of sodomy; and he said and confessed that he had, in a most culpable fashion . . . inflicted on these children various kinds and fashions of tortures, either himself or in the company of his associates, notably the following: Gilles de Sillé, Sir Roger de Briqueville, Henriet and Poitou. They had beheaded the victims with knives, daggers and axes, or had beaten them on the head with batons or other objects, or had hanged them with cord on beams and thus strangled them . . . [Gilles] opened their bodies cruelly, and . . . took pleasure and laughed with the aforesaid Poitou and Henriet, after which he had the bodies burned and reduced to ashes by these two men. Interrogated as to where and when he perpetrated these crimes, and how many there were, he answered: primarily in the Castle of Champtocé, in the year when his grandfather, the Seigneur de la Suze, had died, and that this was where he killed or had killed very many children – the number of which he was no longer certain. And he had committed with them the aforementioned and unnatural crime of sodomy . . . Later, at Nantes in the house which he owned at that time called La Suze he killed, had killed, burned and reduced to ashes a number of children – again he did not know how many – having abused and polluted them, committing with them as before the unnatural crime of sodomy. These crimes were committed entirely for his own wicked pleasure and evil delectation, for no other purpose or intent, and with the counsel of no other person, but following only his own imagination.

Furthermore, the aforesaid Gilles said and confessed that a year and a half past, Eustache Blanchet arranged for M. François Prelati to come from Florence, in Italy, to Gilles, the accused, with the intention of practising diabolical invocation; also that this François had told him that he had found a means in the country which he came from of conjuring up a certain spirit, which then promised him that it would arrange for François to be visited by a demon named Barron, as often as he desired.

And thus Gilles said and confessed that the aforesaid François did indeed carry out various acts of invocation on his orders, either in his presence or when he was absent, and that he, the accused, had been with him for three of these invocations, once at Tiffauges, once at Bourgneuf-en-Rais, and he was unable to recall where the other one took place.

Gilles . . . confessed that to carry out these diabolical invocations they traced signs on the ground in the form of a circle or a cross, with letters. And the aforesaid François possessed a book which he had brought with him from Italy (he said), which contained the names of various demons and the magic words needed to conjure them up, although Gilles could remember neither any of the names nor any of the spells. François had had the book in his hands for the whole two hours of these invocations and conjurations. Gilles affirmed that he, the accused, had never seen or observed a single demon to which he could talk, something which had annoyed him considerably and made him feel cheated.

However, the accused said that during one of the invocations done in his absence, the aforesaid François had, so he told him on his return, seen the demon called Barron and had spoken with him, and the demon had said that he would not appear to Gilles, the accused, because he had not kept his promises. Hearing this, the accused had charged François to ask the demon what he wanted from him, and he had assured him that he would give him whatever he asked for, apart from his soul and his life, provided that the devil would then agree to give *him* what *he* wanted. The accused added that his intention was to ask for knowledge, power and wealth, and to return to the way he was at the beginning of his power and wealth. A little afterwards, François told him that he had spoken to the demon again who, among other things, had demanded that Gilles de Rais give him various limbs from children. After this Gilles gave the aforesaid François the hand, heart and eyes of a young boy, to offer to the demon on his behalf . . .

Deposition of Henriet Griart

Monday, October 17, 1440

. . . when asked what he had done with the bodies and clothes of the murdered children, he replied that he had burned them in the rooms of the accused, Gilles de Rais. Asked how, precisely, he had done this, he said that he had burned the clothes one piece at a time in the fireplace of the aforesaid rooms so that the smell would not be noticed. And to get rid of the bodies, they would lay out great logs, and put the bodies on top of them, then lay sticks on top again, and burn them in that fashion. Asked what he did with the ashes or remains of these burned corpses, he replied that they were hidden in secret places in the rooms where the aforementioned crimes had been committed, or that they were sometimes put into the latrines, or into ditches, or other suitable places . . .

He swore under oath that Catherine, the wife of a certain painter named Thierry, then living in Nantes, had procured and delivered to him her own brother, so that he could take him to Gilles, the accused, in the hope that he might join the chapel school. Henriet went on that he had taken him to Machecoul and into the chambers of Gilles de Rais, and after handing over this child, the accused, Gilles, had made the witness, Henriet, swear that he would never reveal any of his secrets. Asked where he took this oath, he answered that it was in the Church of the Holy Trinity at Machecoul. Asked when, he said that it had been about three years previously,

80

and he also said that after he had handed over the aforesaid child, he had then gone to Nantes, where he had stayed for three days before returning to Machecoul. And when he got back, he searched for the child, but failed to find him, and discovered that the child had, like all the others, left this world. The other witness, Corrillaut (known as Poitou) told him that the accused, Gilles, had killed the child with his own hands; and just like all the others, it had served his libidinous purposes . . .

He swore further that he had at Machecoul seen a young and beautiful boy, page to François Prelati, whose throat had been cut – he did not know by whom, since he had been away at the time. He also swore that Gilles had a sword, of a type called *braquemard* in French, with which he would decapitate or disembowel children . . . He swore further that he had heard Gilles, the accused, say that he had been born under a particular astrological configuration which meant, he said, that no-one could know or understand the perversions or illicit acts that he could be guilty of . . .

He also swore that once in the presence of the accused, Gilles de Rais, and of Eustache Blanchet and of Corrillaut-Poitou, François Prelati had drawn with the point of a sword a great circle on the floor of the great hall in the castle at Tiffauges, and in the four sections had drawn a cross and other signs, on the orders of Gilles, and that then he, Henriet, and the others named had brought in a large amount of charcoal, incense, a magnet, torches and candles, an earthenware pot and other things, which Gilles and Prelati had placed in various parts of the circle. They lit a fire in the pot, then Gilles lit another in the entrance doorway of the hall, and put further signs there and on the walls of the room near the second fire. And then Prelati opened four windows in the form of a cross . . . Then, on the orders of Gilles, the witness and the others withdrew to an upper chamber, taking leave of Gilles and Prelati, who stayed in the hall alone. Gilles formally forbade the witness to reveal anything of what had gone on . . . Later they had heard Prelati speaking in a loud voice, but the witness declared that he had not understood anything that was said. Then the witnesses had heard a noise like a four-footed animal going through the room . . . Asked when this had been, Henriet replied that it had been at night, from just before midnight to about one-thirty . . . The witness also swore that Gilles de Rais and François Prelati were alone at Machecoul for a period of five weeks, in a locked room at the castle, a room for which Gilles never let the key out of his sight; and the witness had heard that in the room a figure of a hand had been found, fashioned in some kind of iron. Still under oath, he added that the accused, Gilles, took into his room at the castle in Tiffauges . . . the heart and hand of a young boy who had been killed on Gilles' orders (or perhaps by Gilles himself), and had put them in a jar covered with a cloth . . . Asked what had been done with this heart and hand, he replied that he was not sure, but that he thought that Prelati and the accused had used them during diabolical invocations, and that they were offering the heart and the hand to the demons they had called up.

Two depositions from witnesses

André Bréchet, of the parish of Ste-Croix in Machecoul, declared under oath that about six weeks earlier he had been on watch at the castle of Machecoul, and just after midnight had fallen asleep; and that when he was asleep, a little man whom he did not recognise came along the road he had been watching, held a naked blade at him and said 'you are dead.' Nevertheless, the man did nothing to him, but went on his way, leaving André in a cold sweat through fear. The next day he met Gilles de Rais coming to Machecoul. After this, he never dared keep watch there again . . . [Various witnesses] declared under oath that one day after Easter last year they had heard Guillaume Hamelin and his wife Ysabeau complain bitterly about the disappearance of two of their children, who were missing. Afterwards they never heard that the children had ever been found or seen again.

Report of the Judgement of the Court

Gilles de Rais was condemned to be hanged and burned . . . [Gilles] made a request to the President of the Court: he and his servants, Henriet and Poitou, had committed enormous and terrible crimes, for which they were condemned to death, and he begged the President that he and his servants should die at the same hour on the same day, but that they should die just after him, who had been the principal cause of their misdeeds . . . for if they did not see him die, they might fall into despair, thinking that they were dying, but that he, the cause of their misfortune, might go unpunished . . . The President agreed to this.

Report of the End of Gilles de Rais

Gilles offered up several fine prayers to God, commending his soul to Him. Then, having given this good example to his servants, he chose to die first. His servants told him to be brave as a knight should, and trust in God's love, and recall the Passion that led to our Redemption. Gilles died in a state of contrition. And before his body was burned, he was cut down and placed in a coffin, and taken to the church of Our Lady of Carmel in Nantes, where he was buried. Then Henriet and Poitou were hanged and burned to ashes. But they had shown much contrition and repented their misdeeds, and they persevered in this until the end.

SOCIETY

This section is inevitably broader than the rest, and it contains a whole rhymed novella about a medieval social climber, delinquent and tearaway. The Middle High German tale of Helmbrecht, a yeoman farmer and his son, was written at the end of the thirteenth century, probably in Bavaria, by Wernher der Gartenaere, who may well have been a Franciscan friar. The whole is an outspoken sermon against the wickedness of modern youth. The writer uses the farmer and his namesake son to contrast old courtly values with the new world at a time when society was breaking down and the feudal system was in decline. There is no doubt at all whose side the writer is on, and the medieval German work is a particularly vivid illustration of a society which is breaking down, with people leaving their proper stations for what are in all senses improper ones. Within the context of the work, the fact that young Helmbrecht gets a particularly horrid comeuppance provides for a satisfactory literary conclusion; but the rather desperate feudal and religious conservatism of the author and his conviction that God's justice will triumph in the end is all a bit optimistic. Historically, of course, even the law enforcement officers (hangmen) can't, couldn't and didn't hold back real social decay for long, and it was a while before the robber-barons and their private armies were brought under control in an empire that by now was well and truly un-holy.

Wernher

Helmbrecht – Father and Son

One man will tell you things that he has seen,
the next of happenings where he has been
a witness. Then again, a third will tell
a tale of love, a fourth of business well–
conducted, and the fifth of property,
then number six of the nobility.
My story is of things well–known to me,
of things that I, with my own eyes, could see.
I saw (and I shall tell you nothing wrong!)
a country farmer's son with hair so long,
so soft and gently curling, that it fell
beyond his shoulders, blond and full as well,
and thus he went – his hair was all his pride.
He kept it dressed and lean, tucked up inside
a hooded cape, embroidered like a book
of stories. I bet you'd have far to look
to see so many birds made out so fair
again! Pigeons and popinjays were there
embroidered well and finished beautifully.
Shall I tell you what else was there to see?

A yeoman farmer – Helmbrecht was his name –
once had a son; he is the very same
lad that this story tells of. His name too
was Helmbrecht, like the father. That the two
should have the same name was the custom then.
So I shall do my best to turn my pen
to show you all, briefly and carefully,
the many wonders that there were to see
upon young Helmbrecht's cape. I'm telling you
that all of this is absolutely true
and I'm not making up a pack of lies.

Right from the back, where the hood starts to rise,

86

up to the top and back, from crown to nape
along the middle seam, young Helmbrecht's cape
had little birds embroidered all around,
as if they'd just alighted on the ground,
having flown there out of the nearby woods
just to come down upon this very hood,
the finest anyone had ever seen,
and far, far better than had ever been
upon this kind of yokel's head! Idiocy!
But – well, let's see what else was there to see.

There was the story of the siege of Troy,
when Paris, that quite impossible boy
stole and seduced the wife of Greece's king,
(a lady he adored above all things),
and how Troy fell after many a day,
and from it how Aeneas fled away
and took to ship, and to the seaways turned,
while at his back the topless towers burned,
and Troy's great walls collapsed, were lost to sight.
Alas, that such a yokel ever might
wear such a cape, embroidered all so well
of which there is so very much to tell.
And now, perhaps, you'd like to hear beside
what was depicted on the other side
with silken threads and wonderful to see?
The tale reports these details honestly.
On Helmbrecht's cape, and all on the right hand
was Charlemagne and his Knight Roland,
and Turpin and Sir Oliver, the four
who fought so hard together, true and sure,
and did heroic deeds of bravery
against the Saracens and their army.
The great lands of Provence, the land of Arles,
fell to the forces of the mighty Charles,
who fought with boldness and with strategy
and with his forces set Galicia free,
a land the pagans held for many a day.

What else was there? One moment, and I'll say.
From one side of the binding to the next
(it's true – all this is in the story's text)
you'll hear what he had tucked behind his ears.
The tale of King Attila's sons was there,
and how they, on Ravenna's battle-field,
each fought so bravely, though each one was killed,
felled by the hand of Witego, the knight,
a brave and wild man, furious in the fight,
who also slew Theoderic the king.

If you like, I can tell you everything
that this young cuckoo had depicted on
his cape. Oh yes, I'll tell you, everyone.

The stupid child had (it's true, I'm bound!)
all down the seam, along and all around
from his right ear and all the way along
behind the left, and round the other one
(I'm sure of this – the story tells me true,
so listen and I'll pass it on to you)
such pictures! Every one a sight to see,
fine knights and ladies, all of chivalry.
Such pictures never ever were surpassed.
And there were lovers there, each with his lass,
outdoors, as they enjoyed a stately tread,
the whole of this picked out in silken thread.
Beside each knight two ladies took their stance
(just as they do today in formal dance).
One knight held firmly to the lady's hand.
And on the cape (embroidered to the end)
between the maidens stood a noble squire
who held *them* by the hand, and rather higher
in the field, well-drawn, a merry fiddler stood,
with other musicians upon that hood.
And now I'll tell you how young Helmbrecht came
to get this cape – the story's very strange.
Helmbrecht – the idiot, the stupid fool!

Yes, how he got it I'll reveal to you.

So let me now narrate for those who hear
the story of the cape itself, and where
it came from. It was all embroidered by
a sexy nun, who fancied chivalry
more than her convent, ran away and fled,
and this is what she got up to instead.
These are strange things for any nun to do,
but, well, I've seen, and it's nothing new!
Her lower abdomen led her astray,
and took her reason with it, so they say.

Helmbrecht had a sister, Gotelind,
and she gave to the nun (she was so kind)
a whole cow for the nun to have as meat.
The nun's embroidery was so neat
that she by needlework earned all her food,
by sewing capes and clothes like Helmbrecht's hood.
So Gotelind gave the nun a whole cow.
But let me tell you what his mother now
gave her – she gave the seamstress-nun
more eggs and cheeses than she'd ever come
by in her convent kitchen in a year;
she'd not have seen so much, or even near.
Indeed, she'd not have had so much good cheese
within those walls – they see nothing like these.
Beside all this, the sister gave Helmbrecht
fine linen, white, the best she could collect,
to make him look his best. No better weave
could be found anywhere. I do believe
that it was woven fine and tightly fit,
and seven weavers worked full time on it
to make a cloth so fine and white and rare,
better than you might come on anywhere.
Still trying to make Helmbrecht look his best,
his mother gave young Helmbrecht even more
to make the son look finer than before:

89

best worsted cloth – no tailor ever held
such cloth to work with in his life; as well
she added in a measure of sheepskin
straight from the animal, as a lining –
the skin was from a pure merino lamb,
and none so white was found in all the land.
The worthy lady also gave the lad
a chainmail coat, the best sword to be had,
and these (the coat of mail and the blade)
gave pleasure to the boy. And then she made
his gear and his accoutrement complete
with all the other things that he thought meet –
a dagger and a leather side-bag – huge
and too absurd for anyone to use!
When they had clothed the boy so very well
he said: 'Mother, now listen and I'll tell
you what I need: a doublet fine and clean.
If I should be without one I shall seem
to be a bumpkin and a nobody.
I know exactly how it ought to be.
It should be such that when you get a sight
of it, you'd say: 'Yes, that will be quite right.'
Your son will do you honour everywhere,
a son who is so noble and so fair.'
So in the clothes-chest that she had at home
there was a cloth-length left, and only one,
and she was sad when she was now required
to sell it for the doublet he desired.
She bought for it some other cloth of blue.
I tell you this – and once more it is true –
that never had a farmer or his type
worn such a cloth, or anything quite like.
Nothing as good as this would ever come their way.
I do assure you that it's true as day!

Whoever told him how to dress up well
certainly knew his stuff! All men could tell
that this lad knew the image he must chance

90

to get from all that much-approving glance.
The doublet was like this: up Helmbrecht's back
right from his belt to the nape of his neck
one button lay close to the next, I'm told,
and every one was shiny, twinkling gold.
So what about it? If you'd like to hear
I'll tell you all about his other gear.

The doublet collar buttoned at the chin
and there were buckles there that kept it in
and they all shone like silver in the sun.
The doublet was the best that anyone
had seen in all their lifetime. Such a one
was never worn by any farmer's son.
Nor had such effort ever gone to waste
in this country, or any other place.
Come on – just have a look at all this gear –
three buttons were of crystal clear,
neatly proportioned all and unsurpassed,
and kept the doublet buttoned fast
for this young idiot, this little loon!
The front of his fine doublet was all strewn
with sequins – you could see them shine and gleam
from far off, blue, yellow and red and green,
or black and white, as he had specified,
and you could see them sparkling far and wide.
They dazzled and they twinkled at a glance
so that, whenever he got up to dance
he was the cynosure of every eye,
and girls and ladies saw him passing by
and followed him with longing, loving looks –
it's true, I tell you! It's all in the book.
And I can tell you something else freely!
Beside *him*, women would not look at me!
And on his bodice, where it joined the sleeves,
right up and down the seams, believe
me, lots of little bells were sewn on here
and you could hear them jingle, loud and clear

when he went dancing, stepping in the line
– a great hit with the ladies every time!
One of the comic poets of yesteryear
could really do this justice, were he here,
better by far than I can manage. Well,
just listen anyway. I've more to tell.

His mother sold plenty of eggs and hens
so that she could buy him some things again –
fine hose, high-buckled shoes were for the boy
to make him even finer, and her joy.
And now he was completely kitted out
and said: 'I want to go off to the court,'
and he went on: 'Dear father, now I need
some help from you, and your support indeed.
My mother and my sister gave me lots
of things – and this shall never be forgot –
for giving me so much you can be sure
they'll have my gratitude for evermore.'
The father was not pleased to hear this said,
but then he thought, and to his son replied:
'You have the clothing. You can have from me
a horse, as proud and fine as he can be,
a jumper or a courser, full of style,
who'll never tire, though you ride many a mile.
This fine beast then will carry you to court
–believe me, it will be most gladly bought,
as soon as I can find one I can buy.
But son, just let me say to you that I
would rather that you gave up all these thoughts
to go and dance attendance at some court.
Please do not go – just listen to my words,
for life at court is very, very hard
for those not born to it – indeed, it's tough
for those who are familiar enough
with it. Son, stay with me and steer the plough,
and saddle up our packhorses, and now
we'll till the land together, you and I,

and live in honour till the day we die,
and you will be my right and proper heir,
esteemed, as I am, honoured everywhere.
I've kept faith with myself and other men,
I've never borne false witness. Always when
I have to pay my tithes each year, I do,
and bring my tributes as and when they're due.
I've lived my life honestly as I can
without envy, with hatred of no man.'

The son said: 'Father dear, I beg of you
not to turn me from what I want to do,
for things cannot be any other way.
I have to go there and I have to stay
and get a taste of how things are at court.
As for those sacks of corn you've always bought,
I'll not be humping them onto my back
or loading dung until my bones all crack,
onto your dung-cart – no, never again,
will you now catch me – never, in God's name,
yoking the oxen up before the plough
sowing the fields and meadows – that I vow!
I tell you father, it would not be fair
on my long, flowing, fine and golden hair
and on my curls and my complexion too,
and on my clothes, so fitting and so new,
and on my cape, the garment that I love,
embroidered all around with silken doves
sewn on it by the ladies. Father, no,
out to the fields I will no longer go!'

The father said: 'Son, stay here by my side
and I shall tell you something else beside.
The Farmer Ruprecht says he'll give to you
his daughter, and some sheep and livestock too,
pigs, and ten cows from his herd, old and younger,
but if you go to court, then you'll feel hunger,
and you won't get soft beds of any sort

and nobody will give you his support.
Just listen to my words – they're fair and true,
and they could mean honour and worth to you.
No one has ever managed yet to last
when he tries moving up out of his class.
Your proper station, son, is at the plough.
You'll meet plenty of gentry anyhow,
and anywhere on earth that you may go
you'll just increase your shamefulness, I know.
My son, I tell you by the Trinity,
at court you'll only be a mockery
for all the proper courtiers. And so,
my son, listen to me and do not go.'

The son replied: 'If I ride there as planned
I'll soon pick up the courtly manners, and
adapt myself to anything I find,
and regular courtiers will never mind,
as soon as they all see my splendid cape
upon my head and shoulders. They'll all gape,
and never in a million years believe
(indeed they never ever could conceive)
that I had ever walked behind the plough
or turned a furrow with the oxen now.
I only have to dress myself well in
fine clothes and all the other splendid things
that I was given by that lovely pair,
mother and Gotelind, my sister fair,
and I shall never – of this I'm quite sure –
be taken for a farm-boy any more.
I'll never look as if I had been born
to till the soil and go and thresh the corn,
or make the flour, or hump the heavy sacks
around the place and nearly break my back.
Now I've a well-turned ankle, and my feet
are shod with slippers that are fine and neat,
my hose are silk, my shoes of finest suède,
so nobody could ever be betrayed

into suspecting me of having toiled
for you or anybody in the fields.
If you would just give me the horse, then I
can bid old Ruprecht a last fond goodbye.
I really do not want to take a wife –
he's lost me as a son-in-law for life!'

The father said: 'Son, just a short while stay
and listen to the things I have to say.
A man who listens to well-meant advice
gets usefulness and respect out of life,
but if a child ignores his parents' plea,
and if he just goes on pigheadedly,
he'll end up on the gibbet, yes he will,
in shame and scandal up on gallows hill.
If you really persist in your intent
and want to match yourself against the men
born rightfully to courtly life, you'll see
that it's a sheer impossibility.
The proper courtier will despise you
(you ought to know by now that this is true)
and then, a farmer never can complain
against a nobleman in law, and win;
but if a courtier robs a farmer, he
might steal from him his total property,
yet in a court he would still win, I'm sure,
more easily than *we* would at the law.
But if you rob the gentry just so you
can eat, my dear son, just make sure you do
not fall into their hands at any time,
or you'll be charged for every single crime
against them, anything that's gone and more,
and you'll not be allowed to plead at law.
Don't be deceived, they soon draw up the bill,
God's on their side, and it will be 'God's will'
if they should kill you when you're in the act.
Well son, there really is no going back.
Stay here and have an honest working life,

live on the farm and take an honest wife.'

He said: 'Father, let things come as they may,
I will not be deflected from the way
I've chosen, living with the noble ones.
I'll leave you here with all your other sons
to toil away behind the plough. The only time
that I'll see cattle is when stealing them,
and driving them away for us to share.
There's only one thing left that keeps me here
and that's the fact I haven't got a steed,
so I can't go out raiding as I need
with all the others, hunting all around
harrying farmers, yes, to cut them down
and drag them through the hedges by the hair.
I can't do that yet, and it isn't fair!
I've simply had enough of being poor
I cannot bear the idea any more
of looking after our sheep and our cow –
that isn't what I wanted anyhow;
no, I want to go thieving every day
so I can get for myself in that way
the sort of food that I should like to eat,
and I can keep the frost off of my feet
and keep myself warm in the winter's chill.
So father, let me beg you, if you will,
to hurry up and go this very day
and see to it – for I'll brook no delay –
and get the horse you said you'd buy for me,
for I can't wait for it eternally!'

I'll try to trim the telling of my tale.
The father had some wool – a good half-bale
(at least that's what is written in my source)
and this wool-bale was very fine, of course,
amongst the best that you would ever need,
and this he sold to buy young Helmbrecht's steed,
but had to add four dairy cows as well,

96

two oxen and three heifers, and to sell
four bushels of his very finest corn.
Alas, that all this useful stuff has gone
to waste. He bought one for ten pounds, you see,
and truth to tell, its value was just three.
That's what he would have got for it at best,
so seven pounds were wasted – all the rest!

But now the son at last was quite ready
to go. He put on all his finery
and then declared – but listen what he said,
shaking his golden and his curly head
so that his hair fell to his shoulders: 'I
could fight a lion, pull stars from the sky,
and I'm in such a ranting, raving mood
I could eat iron bars and call them food.
The emperor would have to call it handsome
if I don't capture him and ask for ransom,
and squeeze a mint of money, vast amounts,
from all the lords and dukes and knights and counts
and viscounts too – I'll kidnap every one,
and rage around the countryside for fun,
with no regard for my own skin at all.
The world's my oyster and I want it all.
And so: dismiss me from paternal care!
From now on I'll be catered for elsewhere.
Father, I tell you in all honesty
a wildman would be easier than me
to rear, a Saxon from the northern wilds.'
The father said: 'I therefore shall, my child
dismiss you from my care here, and I say
I leave you now to fate, to come-what-may.
And since my words were neither here nor there,
and all you think of is your golden hair
which suits your cape – well, take good care of it,
and all those silken doves that on it flit,
that no-one steals it or destroys the thing,
nor damages it, nor causes anything

to happen to all your accoutrements.
And if it still really is your intent
to ignore me and go away from here
for good, I have to tell you that I fear
that you will walk on crutches one fine day
and a small beggar-boy will lead your way.'
Old Helmbrecht went on: 'Son, my dearest boy,
you still could give your parents so much joy
by change of mind. Come, live the way we do,
I and your mother, and I tell you true,
drink water, son, that's honest, clean and fine,
before you rob and steal to get some wine.
I know down south in Austria they may
break the sumptuary laws each day –
not just the fools, even the smarter sort –
they eat and drink far better than they ought.
But you should eat, my son, good honest fare
before you go off robbing anywhere
or steal a cow from someone that you'll swap
to get a chicken dinner. Here we sup
on barley-broth that lasts a week or two,
and that's quite good enough for us – and you!
You ought to eat that kind of healthy course
before you go and steal somebody's horse
and swap that for a roasted goose. My son,
if you would keep my precepts, every one,
you'd live a life of honour and esteem,
a welcome guest wherever you are seen.
My son, eat ryebread, oatmeal porridge, groats,
before you eat a salmon that you've poached.
A thief may not in any honour live –
that's all the teaching that I have to give.
If you should take that message you'll live well.
If not, then that's the very road to hell,
and that's a path you'll have to walk alone.

I can't go with you there – that much I own.
So if you take that path and that descent

98

you'll have to bear the dreadful consequence.'

The son said: 'You drink water, father,
if you like. But wine is what *I'd* rather
take. And you eat up all that old barley,
I tell you, a roast chicken is for me,
and I'll not be told otherwise. White bread
is what I'm going to eat until I'm dead.
Oatmeal is good enough for you and yours,
but I read in the Book of Roman Law
that in youth a child gets all his desires
from his godfather, not his natural sire.
Now my godfather was a noble knight
(a man of worthy standing in God's sight);
I have nobility in me through him, I swear,
so I can aim so high in my career.'

The father said: 'Believe that if you will.
I know that I would rather honour still
someone who knew his place within God's scheme,
and stayed there, sticking to this way of things.
Even if he were born in lowly state,
amongst the people he'd more highly rate
than somebody of royal birth, who'd use
his power and privilege to abuse.
If you should place a man, low-born but true
beside a man of better stock, but who
has no esteem whatever of his own,
and put them somewhere where they're both unknown,
then folk will always place the low-born child
above the one who's better-born, but wild,
the one who chose to live a life of shame
rather than live up to his noble name.
Son, if you want to be a noble man
I'll give the best advice I ever can:
just *act* as nobly as you think you might.
For real nobility – you'll see I'm right –
lies in noble behaviour, nothing more.

This is the truth; of nothing I'm more sure.'

Young Helmbrecht said: 'Father, your words are fair
indeed. My fine cape and my lovely hair
and all my clothes, all done in such good taste,
mean that I cannot stay here in this place.
My clothes, which draw every admiring glance,
just need to be shown off at some great dance,
and not be used to plough the filthy earth.'

'Alas that your mother ever gave birth
to you, my son,' the father said.
'You miss what's good, go for the bad instead.
Son, you are still a fine, well-built young man,
so tell me just one thing if you but can
(that is, if you should have just enough wit):
who lives a better life, this man or that –
the one upon whom curses always fall,
and who brings damages to one and all,
and causes suffering and fear and pain,
paying no heed to God's great holy name –
does that one lead a better life than he
pwho differs from this very thoroughly,
a man useful to others in his deeds,
who tries his best and usually succeeds
in helping people by day and by night,
and who keeps God's commandment in his sight,
so everywhere he finds himself on earth,
God and the people all respect his worth?
Dear son, what I should like you now to do
is tell me honestly, and tell me true
which of the men that I have placed before
you – which of them pleases you more?'

'Dear father, surely it is very clear –
the man who does no mischief is more dear
because he gives his fellow-men his aid;
yes, surely he lives better in all ways.'

100

'My own dear son – you could be like that too
if you'd listen to all I've said to you.
All you need do is plough and dig like me,
and you'll be useful to society.
That way you'd benefit the human race
both rich and poor, and you'd enjoy their grace
and all God's creatures then would know your worth –
the wolf, the eagle, everything on earth
that God has put there for the use of man,
called into being as only He can.
My son, my son, just stay and plough the field!
Lords and ladies are raised up from its yield –
society rests upon the farmer's toil,
even the emperor owes his crown as well
to all the farmer's labours and his tithes;
no other worker could be set so high.
Yes, all the empire's glory were as nought,
but for the land and the farmer's support.'

Young Helmbrecht said: 'Father, don't preach to me!
Enough of all your sermons! I can see
that you should really be a preacher, too –
your homilies would surely get a few
hundred to go on a pilgrimage each time,
off to Jerusalem and to the holy shrine.
But listen, father, what I want to say
is this: when farmers work so hard today
it only means that they eat all the more.
Whatever shall befall me, I'm quite sure
that farming really holds nothing for me,
and if I have to soil my hands, you see,
by following the plough, then you should know
that I'd betray myself on earth below
and also God above! A sad mischance,
if a *ploughman* led a lady out to dance.'

The father said: 'Now just ask yourself this
and try and work out what the answer is,

as if you were amongst wise men, my lad,
and tell the meaning of a dream I had.
I saw you with two torches in your hand
that burned so brightly that the very land
was dazzled with their radiance and gleam.
But son, just then I had another dream
(a while ago) – I dreamed about someone
who walked a poor blind beggar in the sun.'
Young Helmbrecht said: 'Father, that's as may be,
no story like that ever will set me
against my plans for what I have in mind.
I'd have to be one of the weakest kind!'
The father's warning being thus ignored,
old Helmbrecht went on: 'Son, I dreamed much more;
I dreamed you limped everywhere on one leg
and for the other had a wooden peg
that stuck out from your garment down below,
and had to hobble everywhere you'd go.
I tell you, take not of this other dream,
and ask of wiser people what it means.'

The son said: 'It means only that I'm right
for earthly joys and heavenly delight.'
The father said: 'But there is even more,
another dream, one far worse than before.
I saw you over hills and woods, flying,
but men then tore from you one of your wings,
ripped it clear from you, and with that your flight
was broken, and you fell into the night.
Now what of *this* dream – can that be good news?
Alas, for all the limbs that you could lose!'
'Father, father, all these dreams you see
mean nothing but joy and delight for me.'
With that the youth said: 'What you must do now
is find somebody else to steer your plough,
because you're wasting time for both of us
with all these dreams and all this fearful fuss.'
Old Helmbrecht said: 'Son, never mind *those* dreams!

I had one more. Just think what this one means,
a dream the like of none I've had before.
It seemed to me that in my sleep I saw
you by a tree and – now, this is the worst –
light could be seen between your feet and earth,
while on a branch, where you were down below,
a raven sat, and next to him a crow.
Your hair was wild, and blowing far and wide
were bits torn out of it from either side;
on one side there the raven sat and hacked,
while on the other was the crow so black.
Alas, my son, such visions I should see!
Alas, my son, the horrid gallows-tree!
Alas the raven, and alas the crow!
That dream just spells disaster – this I know,
and I have let you grow up so unwise,
unless it be the dream is all pure lies.'

'Father, father, in Christ's name I declare,
you can dream anything you like or care,
both good and evil, any kind of thing.
You'll not dissuade me from my travelling.
I swear it's true, and hope that I may die
if I were unsure of my destiny.
Father, I leave. May God watch over you
and also over my dear mother too,
and may the blessing of the Lord of All
rest on the other children, great and small,
and may God keep us all till Judgement Day.'
With that he took his horse and rode away.
He took leave of his father, then he spurred
his horse across a gate, into the world.
If I would try to tell you what befell
him after that, and all his doings – well,
it would take me a good three days or more,
and probably a week, of that I'm sure.
He rode until he reached a castle where
the overlord had just one single care:

warfare, a robber-baron through and through,
always willing to take on someone new
provided he was well prepared to ride
and fight with all and sundry, at his side.
He took young Helmbrecht in to join his band
and go out robbing wildly through the land,
and Helmbrecht soon became the worst of all,
who stole things that the others might let fall,
–not him! It all went into Helmbrecht's bag,
nothing was so small that he did not grab
it, nor was anything of such great size
that Helmbrecht would not claim it as his prize;
rough, smooth, bent, straight, or long or short –
young Helmbrecht took the lot without a thought.
The son of Farmer Helmbrecht – honest man –
just stole it all; he took the horses and
he took the cows, and never left a thing.
He took fine swords and then he took jerkins,
he took folk's cloaks and then he took their coats,
he took their cattle and he took their goats
he took the ewes, he took the rams beside
(and one day he paid for it with his hide!)
but now he stole the skirts of ladies fair,
from off their very bodies everywhere
and all their robes and also all their furs
(and one day he got something rather worse
when the hangman at last caught up with him,
and then he wished he'd left the ladies' things!)
I do assure you that my story is quite true!

Now all through that first year a fair wind blew
for him, and filled his sails fully, so
it took his ship where he wanted to go.
Too soon his confidence (that above all)
meant that he grabbed the best part of each haul,
the lion's share of everything they stole.
But then one day he thought that he should go
back home; some instinct must have led him on

to think about his family, where he'd come from.
And so he took his leave, both from his lord
and from his thieving friends, and with a word
he blessed them as he set out the next day,
that God protect them while he was away.

And now occurred some very curious things,
events that are so very interesting
that they must now all be passed on to you.
I only hope that my poor skills will do
justice to how young Helmbrecht found the farm.
Did they welcome him? Yes, with open arms.
All ran towards him, jostling in a race
to see this young man come back to the place.
Each of the household hurried to the fore,
father and mother as never before
running (faster than to tend a sick cow!)
but who would win, and claim the first gift now?
The groom reached him first, and he got his share –
a fine shirt and some breeches, a fine pair.
Now, did the women and the steward come
and shout 'Young Helmbrecht, welcome home?'
Not really. What they did I'll tell you true.
Since this seemed not the proper thing to do,
their words of greeting all were rather more
effusive: 'Pray be welcome, noble sir.'
He said: '*A braw guid nicht to ane an' a,
and may the guid lord keep ye evermair.*'
Young Helmbrecht's sister then came to the place
and put her arms around him in embrace.
With this young Helmbrecht spoke now to his sister
and said (another language!): '*gracia vester.*'
The younger folk had rushed to meet the son,
and after them the elders, one by one
were greeted by him most expansively.
To Farmer Helmbrecht he said '*deu sal*' grandly
(in Portuguese!). His mother came along
and he said '*dobra ytra*' in the Slavic tongue.

105

So now the folk all stared at one another,
young Helmbrecht's old father and his mother.
The wife said: 'Husband, I very much fear
that we are all sadly mistaken here.
This visitor is not our child Helmbrecht,
he sounds to be a Slovene or a Czech!'
The father said: 'No, this is some Frenchman,
and hence the son that went away, this can
not be – I am as sure of that as anything,
although he really looks a lot like him.'
Gotelind, Helmbrecht's sister spoke, and she
agreed that this man simply could not be
the son: 'He spoke Latin to me at least.
It's my opinion that he'll be a priest.'
The groom then spoke up: 'No, I'm sure he's not.
To me he sounded something like a Scot,
or someone from up North of here, I know.
That's where their speech is accented and slow,
say, Sweden, Saxony or somewhere similar,
at least it's possible he comes from there.
He said 'a braw guid nicht' to me at first –
I'll bet he is a Scotchman at the worst!'

Old Helmbrecht now came up to him and said:
'If you *are* young Helmbrecht my son, instead
of these words, speak some of our language, come,
the language we have always used at home,
so that I understand who you may be
and you will then have done convincingly.
You say things like '*deu sal*' – nonsense, it seems,
and we have no idea what that might mean.
Come, show respect to mother and to me
and for that you will gain our sympathy.
just speak a word or two of German, and
I'll tend your horse for you with my own hand –
yes, I shall do it, for no groom I'll call,
if you are my son Helmbrecht after all,
and welcome you back to our home today.'

106

'You grubby little peasant, keep away,
and that common old woman there beside!
My mount, my splendid prancer and my pride
shall never ever, and I tell you true,
be handled by someone as coarse as you.'

Farmer Helmbrecht was shaken, but his words
were kind against the insult he had heard:
'If you are really Helmbrecht, it is right
that we should have roast chicken here tonight,
but if you are not our son Helmbrecht, then,
some Slav perhaps, or a Bohemian,
then go off to Bohemia and your kind,
for I've enough to do with me and mine
to keep us happy, well and healthy too.
Priests only get just what to them is due,
precisely what I owe, no less, no more.
So if you are not Helmbrecht, then be sure
you won't sit at my board or share our food –
it's quite impossible. It is no good –
however much I had, and of what worth,
if you're a Saxon, or come from up North,
or if you are a Frenchman, well, I'd say
that you'll have brought provisions for your way,
and you'll have with you everything you need,
because from me you'll get nothing indeed.
However long the night, you won't be able
to get a single scrap from off my table.
I've got no beer, mead, wine or all the rest;
young lord, go to the nobles as their guest!'

By now the night was really drawing on.
Young Helmbrecht thought he had been there too long
to move now, so he said: 'In God's own name
I shall be glad to tell you who I am
and what they call me, for I see
there's no-one near whose hospitality
I could enjoy. He thought, 'a poor idea

107

to use my foreign languages down here.
It really hasn't been much use to me,
and so I guess I'll have to let it be.'
Aloud he said: 'Yes, father, I'm your son.'
The father said: 'So name yourself. Which one?'
'The one whose name is just the same as yours.'
'So tell me, I must hear it to be sure.'
'Helmbrecht's my name – the child you must know.
I worked for you here just a year ago.
This is the truth, of this you can be sure;
my name is Helmbrecht. I can say no more.'
The father said: 'No, this I can't believe.'
'It's true!' 'So you will simply have to give
the names of our four oxen, every one,
then I'll believe that you can be my son.'
'I shall be glad to do so; for besides
I've often used my stick across their hides.
Your lead-ox is called Toughie, and he'd be
well-valued in the whole community
on any farm. The richest in the land
would be well pleased to have that one on hand.
The second is called Rammer, but his name
deceives, because he's really pretty tame,
no milder ox was ever yoked to plough.
The third one I shall name for you right now
and he's called Ernest – it's all in my brain,
and I can call them up for you again
and name them for you, every single one.
Now must I prove again that I'm your son?
The fourth ox in the team is Sunny Jim,
so if I've named them all well – also him –
then take me in and let me be your guest,
so I can come indoors and take my rest.'
The father said: 'Here in the cold outside
my son, you need no minute longer bide.
Come in, come in, my doors and pantries too
will all be open now and free to you.'

You know, fate really is a fickle jade!
For I can say that in all my born days
I've never had quite such a reception
as now was given to the errant son.
His horse was led away, watered and fed
while he was found the softest of all beds –
see how his sister and his mother dote!
The father gave the horse a mass of oats
and didn't stint the measure by a jot
(I'm sure they'd never give *me* such a lot
if I turned up at some place unannounced,
and wanted looking after! Not a chance!)
The mother shouted to her daughter busily:
'Run to the linen cupboard now and find for me
a bolster and a pillow, soft and plump,
as quickly as you can, jump to it, jump!'
They settled him on cushions just above
the warmest place by their great central stove,
where he could simply take his ease and wait
till it was time for everyone to eat.
He dozed in comfort, lying warm and still
till it was time for them to start the meal.
He washed his hands, sat down, and they began.
Now listen, I'll say how the menu ran!
I'll tell you what came first upon that table
and if I were a lord, then I'd be able
to eat such dishes, prepared in this way,
myself, at my own table, every day.
Vegetables were chopped and well prepared
and, lean and juicy, on them was laid there
a splendid, thick and well-cooked piece of meat.
Now hear what next the people got to eat:
a large full-fat soft cheese was quickly served
but then came the veritable *chef-d'oeuvre*.
Now, how is this for culinary news!
There'd never ever been a fatter goose
well-roasted over fires on the spit
(they did it gladly; no-one grudged a bit

to welcome Helmbrecht back into the fold).
The goose was massive (that's what I've been told)
much like a bustard – this they now put out
for hungry young Helmbrecht to set about.
They also had a chicken-roast, and stew,
as farmer Helmbrecht ordered his cook to.
The meal was served up for Helmbrecht's delight –
a noble lord would glory in the sight
if he sat in his hunting-lodge at ease
and he were given dishes such as these.
Course after course came in, all this and more,
a yeoman's table never saw before
the great delights they set before the son
for his enjoyment, each and every one.

The father said: 'If I had any wine,
believe you me, tonight would be the time
I'd drink it. But, dear son, you must not mind
drinking spring water of the finest kind
that ever might be drawn out of the earth.
I know of few springs that could match its worth,
apart from one a mile or so away,
but no-one brings that water here today.'
When they had eaten and enjoyed their fill,
old Helmbrecht could resist no more: 'Now, tell
me, son, tell me about the court and say
how they all spend their time from day to day,
and then I'll tell you how it used to be –
at least, I'll show you how it seemed to me
when I was young and used to visit them –
how men behaved at court away back then.'
'Father, do tell me all you want to say,
then I'll say what the court is like today.
Just ask me anything you want to know –
I tell you how it is and what we do.'

'A long way back, when I was just a lad
working for old Helmbrecht – your grandad,

my father, that is, named like me and you –
he sent me to the court to pay our dues.
I had to take a tithe of eggs and cheese
the way a yeoman farmer always does,
and there I got to see the knights at play
and watched the way that they behaved all day.
They were all courtly, genteel and polite
and free of all the wickedness that quite
spoils them today – you see it everywhere,
alas, in all the men and women there.

The knights all enjoyed one custom the most –
they all engaged in sport and at the joust;
the ladies all looked on in pure delight
(a courtier once explained to me the sights
when I asked him about these doings, all,
and what the various sports and games were called).
The knights – if all my memories are true –
would form two equal groups, and then the two
would ride against each other on the field
and each would try to make the other yield.
Of course, you know that in our social class
such fierce activities don't come to pass
as those I saw there going on at court
(but still, indeed, all this is as it ought
to be). And after all these things were done
a stately formal dance was then begun
with lively singing and with music gay
and merrily the hours then passed away.
First a musician came into the ring
and he began a lively fiddling.
The ladies stood up in their finery
–now that was an impressive sight to see! –
and all the knights approached them, treading sure,
and took their hands, and led them to the floor.
I say again – that was a sight to see! –
the ladies, and the flower of chivalry.
Just watching them was like a magic charm,

young nobles, all with ladies on their arm
advancing merrily and happily,
the highest, and lesser nobility.
And when the stately dance was over, then
a bard came forward from the waiting men
and sang a tale of heroes for the rest,
while others did just what they liked the best,
each carried on with some activity;
one group, perhaps, practised their archery
and shot their arrows at a target true,
while others all found splendid things to do.
Some set off for the hunt. But I must say
the worst of them would be the best today.
I saw in those days – yes, I really knew –
what reputation, faith and honour do,
but now the whole world's full of wickedness,
and cheats and villains flourish in excess,
and have destroyed the things that used to be,
and wrecked the good, and turned things terribly
with all their evil tricks and wicked ways.
These were the sort that nobles in those days
would not let near the court, or take them in;
but nowadays it's quite a different thing.
You count at court as noble, great and wise
if what you're good at is malice and lies.
At court you're worthy, and have more esteem
(far more than I should ever really dream
was possible) than many an honest man
who honours God and does the best he can.
That's what I know of how it used to be.
Now son, perhaps you'll do the courtesy
of telling me how things are there today?'

'Gladly I will. Listen to what I say.
Well. At the court today you'll hear the words
'come on and drink, drink, drink, my noble lords,
if you drink that, I'll match you to the drop,
let's swill and slurp and never ever stop.'

112

That's true. And now I'll tell you all the rest.
There used to be folk of the very best
type there, and all those noble ladies too.
You only find the people now (it's true!)
down at the vintners, when they're selling wine.
You see, that's what is always on our mind
from dawn to dusk, from morning until night,
whether the wine will last us out alright,
and if it does, how can the court get hold
of more good stuff, rich, fruity, red and old,
to match that which we've swilled the livelong day,
which makes us merry, lively, blithe and gay.
We have genteel endearments, that is true –
like: 'Fill the wine cup, little darling, do!'
But now you'd look an idiot, a chump,
to court a lady, when you could get drunk.
Good liars, now – they have the pride of place,
and treachery counts as a special grace,
confidence tricksters – yes, we need them, too,
and anyone who knows a dodge or two.
If you swear like a sailor when he's mad,
then we say: 'Now that's what I *call* a lad!'
All that old-fashioned rubbish you describe,
we've dumped all that, it's gone and more beside.
The folk who live like you we all ignore
and no-one pays attention any more –
they'd be about as welcome at our gates
as, say, the executioner and his mates.
But then, we only laugh at all the law.'
The old man said: 'God help you evermore!
Alas that evil should have spread abroad.'
'All that old jousting – that's gone by the board,
and we've got new games now. They used to say:
'Up sirs, most noble knights, and to the sword!'
What you hear now all day's a different word:
'Quick, steal that cattle, grab it and get back.
Spear him or slash him down, hack, hack!
Take that old fool and put out both his eyes.

113

Cut that one's feet off, chop him down to size.
And as for that one, we'll just see him hang,
then go and find some other wealthy man
who'll pay a fortune if we let him go.'
This is the kind of daily life I know.
Dear father, listen, if I wanted to
then I could tell a thousand tales to you
about the way we live and how we keep.
But now I'm tired, and really need to sleep.'

And so they did as the young Helmbrecht said,
and everything was then prepared for bed.
They spread a linen coverlet for him
(brought to him by his sister, Gotelind)
over the bed-place where he took his ease
after his travels to his father's house.
And so he slept through till the next mid-day.
Of what he did then, I'll have more to say.

A visitor – this rule is always true,
and Helmbrecht kept up with the practice, too –
brings presents when he comes to see people.
He brought the family a whole bag-full,
for mother, father and his sister too.
If I now tell you what they were, then you
will all be very much amused to hear
what Helmbrecht brought them back after this year.
He brought his father a sharpening-stone.
No-one would ever find a better one
to use when he went out to cut the hay.
He also brought a scythe. Again, I say
no better one could possibly be found,
and what a gift to give a farmer, now!
He also brought an axe. I need not tell
that this was of the finest sort as well –
no smith had ever made a better – and
lastly he put an adze into his hands.
What he brought home and gave to his mother

was a full coat made of the finest fur
(but he himself, young Helmbrecht had, alas,
stolen it from a priest during a mass).
Yes, if the goods were stolen, be assured
that I shall tell you – I give you my word.
Helmbrecht had stolen *everything*! I know
he'd robbed a merchant not too long ago
and got a bolt of silk of some great cost,
which now to Gotelind he lightly tossed,
together with a band so rich and rare
that only nobles are allowed to wear
according to the sumptuary law,
and not a farmer's daughter, that's for sure!
The groom was given shoes with leather ties –
Helmbrecht had judged and he had got his size
for him, and he had chosen them with care
and brought them with him all the way from there.
Helmbrecht was now so very upper-crust
that now he clearly felt he really must
give the lad shoes – he'd gone barefoot before.
The maid he gave a fine silken head-square
and an embroidered cloth, soft to the touch,
and both these rich gifts pleased her very much.

Well now, the time has come for us to say
how long young Helmbrecht decided to stay
there. In fact it was just a week, I fear,
but to young Helmbrecht it felt like a year
since he had been out on a robbing raid,
and so he took his leave, no longer stayed
there with father and mother, but was gone.
'No,' said his father: 'No, my own dear son,
if you can live the way we've treated you
this week, then I urge you to stay – please do,
we'll give you all the things that you have seen
if you stay here, and you keep your hands clean.
Son, stop this decadent behaviour,
give up the court, come back and farm once more.

The life at court is bitterness, I fear;
I'd rather be an honest farmer here
than be a petty courtier without
any real rights or lands to boast about,
and who must risk his life, and fight and ride
to battle always at some patron's side,
and always has, at any time of day
the clear awareness that perhaps he may
be captured by his enemies, that he
may lose a limb, or be hanged from a tree.'
'Father,' the young man said, 'I know you care,
and what you have in mind is my welfare,
and I am grateful for it, you are kind.
But still, I haven't had a drop of wine
for seven whole days now! Besides, I've felt
the need to tighten by three holes my belt.
I've really got to go and catch a steer
and eat it very quickly too, I fear,
to get my belt back to its former place
and not pull it so tightly round my waist.
There are some farmsteads I must see to, and
some cattle that will come into my hands
before I can take any more time off
and I'll make sure then that I eat enough.
For instance, a rich man, not far away,
insulted me in the worst of all ways,
the very thought leaves me with anger filled –
he rode across one of my patron's fields!
Now if I can just lay my hands on him
he'll pay for it a thousand times again.
We'll have his cattle, each and every beast,
his sheep and goats and pigs – the very least
that he can do to expiate his crime
of riding through my patron's field that time –
I tell you, when I think what he did there,
the insult really is too much to bear.
And there's another rich man I could name
and he insulted me the very same

116

way – *for he dipped his cake into his drink*!
I'll die before I let *that* go, I think!
And there's a third rich man that I can see,
whose insult was the worst of all the three,
an insult greater than I've ever heard;
and even if the bishop interfered
I wouldn't let it go at all, I swear;
his insult really was too much to bear.'
The father asked: 'What did this rich man do?'
'He opened up his belt a notch or two
when he sat there at table with us all.
If I catch up with him he's going to fall,
and every single thing the fellow owns
I'll have off him, and never mind his moans.
The oxen that he used to draw his plough
I shall convert into hard cash, and now
this will help me to look even more fine –
and I shall dress very well at the time
when we come to have our great Christmas feast.
I think that this would be the very least
that I can do. Come on, what was the fool
thinking of, and the many others too
who have insulted me and caused me pain?
I must take my revenge on them again,
or I'd be held a coward back at home.
You know, one wretched fellow blew the foam
off of his beer when I was near one day.
For that the fool is really going to pay
or else I'll have no standing any more
before the ladies, as I did before,
nor yet be fit to buckle on a sword!
Oh yes, before too long you'll all get word
of Helmbrecht and of all his mighty deeds,
how he mowed down a whole farmstead, like weeds.
And even if the man himself should flee,
I'll make sure that his cattle come with me.'

The father said: 'My son, before you go,

one other thing I'd really like to know
is what your friends are called, the fellows who
taught all these manners and these tricks to you,
that you should seek out men who are quite rich,
and rob them then of every single stitch
because they dip their cake into the pot!
Tell me their names – I'd like to know the lot.'

Helmbrecht said: 'There's my good friend Filch-a-lamb,
and his companion, who's called Eat-a-ram.
These two taught me most of the things I do,
but there are others I'll name for you too.
Swag-bag is one, and Rattle-safe as well –
they taught me more than I can tell.
Cow-gobbler too, Toss-pot's another one –
these, father, are my companions,
I spend all of my time with these young men,
and I have named the six finest of them.
And then there's Wolf-throat! Anyone can see,
however much he loved his family,
aunts, cousins, nephews – still I know
he'd happily turn them out in the snow
without a stitch of clothing to their name –
strangers and relatives, it's all the same.
And then there's Wolf-snout too; the locks
on money chests and any kind of box
all fall to him. Once in a single year I saw
him crack apart a hundred locks or more
that otherwise had held fast. They simply spring
open, if he but comes near to the thing.
But that's his *special* skill; I'll leave aside
the horses, oxen and the cows beside
that he has cleared from local farms as well;
just how many there are I couldn't tell.
At any rate, the locks gave up the ghost
when he came near, and then he took the most.
And then there is another pal of mine,
a noble youth, who carries such a fine

name, better than most other names I know
(a duchess gave it to him long ago,
a noble and a richly endowed dame):
Sir Twytte of Twyttersville's his name,
although we call him Wolfsgut hereabouts.
In any kind of weather he'll be out
on robbing-raids – he never gets enough,
and thieving, well, that is the very stuff
he likes the best, he's never satisfied,
and certainly he never will decide
to give the bad up and go for the good;
such an idea would never match his mood.
Indeed, to go out thieving is a need
he feels, like crows want new-sown seed.'

The father said: 'After that, tell me, do,
the name these people have given to you,
with all these fellows and brothers-in-crime,
what name have they given to you this time?'
'Dear father, ᵀ shall let you know my name –
indeed it doesn't cause me any shame:
and Gobble-goods is what they all call me.
The local farmers are not pleased to see
me coming – for they all soon come to know
that now the children all will have to go
on bread and water diets at the best;
and I put them to many other tests –
in one case, say, a farmer's eye I'll poke,
or maybe hang him up over the smoke,
I'll stake another one on an anthill,
and others, too, with pincers then I will
pull out their beards, and do so bit by bit,
or pull their hair out, every scrap of it.
Sometimes I like to rearrange a face,
or hang them up in some secluded place
by their heels, dangling from a tree,
for what the farmers have belongs to me!
When all ten of us ride out from the wood,

119

even twenty defenders are no good;
and after all, we're fighting for our pride,
so we take them all on and more beside.'

Old Helmbrecht said: 'My son, these friends of yours,
I'm sure you know them very well, and more
than I do, my dear child. But even yet,
wild as these men might be, I still would bet
that God's great justice will prevail at last,
and then the hangman's chains will hold them fast,
and he will have the last word in the game –
if they are ten or thirty, all the same.'
The son said: 'Father, I *shall* change my way,
stop doing what I've done up till today,
and I'll not be persuaded otherwise.
Geese, hens and chickens and other supplies,
and cattle, cheese, and all your dairy stuff
I've managed to preserve often enough
and spare what's owned by you and by my mother,
and got the lads to go and raid some other;
but even though I've kept them off before,
I don't think I shall bother any more.
For all this claptrap you spout without end
is quite insulting to my noble friends,
they are a fine and an upstanding lot,
and if they rob and thieve a bit, so what?
Your pious stuff has quite spoiled my day,
you should have kept your mouth shut anyway!
If you had done so, then I'd have been kind
and married off my sister Gotelind
to my friend Filch-a-lamb, to be his wife,
and then she could enjoy a splendid life,
the best that any woman in the wide world can,
when wed to such a very splendid man.
Fur tippets, linen, cloaks and other clothes
(the local church has good supplies of those)
she would have got them from him, everything,
had your cruel judgements not had such a sting

120

and wounded me so deeply. Gotelind
would certainly have found my friend so kind
that she (if she'd agreed to be his wife)
could eat roast beef every day of her life.'
But then he said to Gotelind: 'My dear
sister, Filch-a-lamb chanced one time to hear
about you, and then begged me for your hand
in marriage. I was much in favour, and
told him that if both you and he agree,
then this would be acceptable to me,
that he would have no cause ever to rue
the match – I knew you to be good and true,
so he need not have the anxiety
that if he fetched up on the gallows-tree
you would not come to him and cut him down,
and lay your husband's body in the ground
at some remote crossroads along the way,
and you'd bring myrrh and incense every day
and night for one whole year, and that you would
tend to his grave and let him rest in peace,
I'm sure for him that you would do all this!
I said: 'My noble sister, later on
would one day even keep your skeleton.
And if by chance the verdict's milder, and
you only lose your eyes, then by the hand
she'll lead you over meadows, paths and stiles,
and help you cover all the weary miles.
And if you have one foot cut off instead
she'll bring your crutches to you in your bed
on each and every morning of the year,
oh yes, she'll do that for you, never fear;
and if it isn't just a foot you lose,
but they should hack the hand off that you use,
she'll cut your meat up and she'll slice your bread
until the day that both of you are dead.'
When I said this, old Filch-a-lamb told me:
'If Gotelind, your sister, is happy
to take me, what a dowry I shall give,

so she in greatest luxury shall live.
I've got three sacks of plunder by me still,
and all so heavy that you'd think them filled
with lead. The first of these three sacks has got
the finest uncut linen – and a lot!
If you sold it, it wouldn't be too hard
to get at least a guinea for a yard –
I'm sure she'd relish such as gift as that.
I'll tell you what is in the second sack –
it's crammed with blouses, skirts and lingerie;
she'd never feel the bite of poverty
if I became her husband, she my wife,
I'd settle all my goods on her for life
the day after the wedding, that I'd do,
and let her have my other plunder, too.
My third sack's crammed full to the very brim
(so much so that I can get no more in)
with shawls and furs and other cloth as well,
and two of them – now this I'm proud to tell –
are lined with scarlet, deep and red and rich,
and all around the edges has been stitched
a trim of sable fur along the seam.
I hid the lot in a nearby ravine,
so I can very quickly get it back
and give her it tomorrow, every sack!'
That's what he said – but father's scotched it all
with his harsh words, so Gotelind, farewell;
I greatly fear you'll have a bitter life
if you should end up as the lawful wife
of some old farmer – he'll be quite a boor,
and it's the wife that suffers, that's for sure.
You'll have to work for him right from the dawn
till dusk, hump sacks and help him thresh his corn,
and dig the turnip-fields laboriously!
My Filch-a-lamb would have spared you drudgery,
my noble and my very worthy friend.
Alas, my lovely sister Gotelind,
the idea causes me a lot of pain

that I should see you when we meet again
wed to some ugly oafish farmer, who
will press unwelcome affections on you,
then fall asleep and snore the night away.
Alas, my sister, how I rue the day
when that father of yours was so unkind –
and by the way, he's no father of mine!
I'll tell you this quite confidentially,
that in her fifteenth week of pregnancy
when my mother was having me, she lay
secretly with a nobleman one day,
who came along and slipped into her bed,
and so I now take after him instead,
and also from my godfather – fine man –
whom God preserve for just as long He can,
it's all through these two men, I feel,
that my behaviour's noble and genteel.'

When she heard this, his sister Gotelind
said: 'There's one thing I've always had in mind,
that really I am not his daughter either,
because a noble knight seduced my mother
when I was in her womb. The knight was very bold
and took my mother outside in the cold
when she was looking for a cow that strayed.
So this explains why I'm so nobly made.
Dear brother Gobble-goods, I ask of you,
(and may the good Lord see that it comes true)'
thus spoke the sister Gotelind,
'That in view of all this, you'll be so kind
and give me Filch-a-lamb to be my man.
That way I'll always have food in my pan,
I'll have the pick of fine wines everywhere,
and my store-cupboard never will be bare,
and I'll have all the beer I need around,
and fine white flour, wonderfully ground.
And if I get those sacks of his, all three,
then I'll be free of any poverty –

I shall have things to eat and things to wear,
of everything I'll have my proper share,
and I'll have everything that a wife should
get from her husband in the way of goods.
And what's more, I know I can offer him
just what he needs – yes, I know I can bring
my body, I've got everything he'll need!
If only our wretched father agreed!
Besides, I'm quite three times as tough, you know
as my sister, who married long ago,
and on the morning after, no-one said:
'Let's help the poor thing get out of her bed.'
The bedding didn't kill her, we could see,
and I'm quite sure that no more will it me,
unless I really have misheard the facts
and it involves some rather different acts.
Dear brother Helmbrecht, please do hear me out
(and what I say you must not spread about);
let me come with you on the narrow track
out through the pine-forest, when you go back,
you see, I really, truly want to wed
your friend and lie beside him in the bed.
For that I'm quite prepared to risk the lot,
father and mother and the home I've got.'

Of this new plan the father got no wind,
nor did the mother guess what was in mind,
but the brother and sister soon agreed
on their next moves, and settled with all speed
that she should run away like him some day.
'And then I'll see you're married straightaway
to my friend Filch-a-lamb – he'll lie with you
no matter what your father tries to do.
To have a man like that's what you deserve,
and you'll be rich if such a man you serve.
So if, sister, your resolve is true
I'll send a messenger who'll come to you
for you to follow him – he'll lead you on,

so you and Filch-a-lamb can become one.
I'm sure that this plan of mine will succeed
for both of you, and you'll have all you need.
I shall arrange a wedding feast with guests
who will bring finery, the very best
of clothes and ornaments, all for your use –
yes, I shall do that for you in all truth.
Now sister, make sure you are all prepared,
and I'll make sure that Filch-a-lamb is squared
as well. God bless you now! I must away.
Or else my welcome (so-called) I'll outstay
from father. Mother, blessings on your head.'
And so off on his old path he then sped,
and brought the news to Filch-a-lamb with pride
that Gotelind agreed to be his bride.
His friend, delighted, kissed young Helmbrecht's hand
a thousand times, embraced him fondly, and
said that he blessed the air, the blessed wind
that had been breathed by lovely Gotelind.

But now the story takes a sorry turn.
Many widows and orphans had to learn
to live without things that were stolen now,
and cope with this new tragedy somehow,
when Filch-a-lamb, young Helmbrecht's mighty friend,
got married to the lovely Gotelind,
and they sat in the seat of honour there.
The food they ate was brought from everywhere
around, they fetched it all from far and wide;
for days on end the men would ride and ride
to bring the things they wanted. Day and night
they worked to make the wedding feast quite right.
Food came in cartloads, and on horses too,
at every hour of the day. And soon
The bridegroom's father's house was full of food.
I'm sure the wedding-spread was not as good
when Arthur (mighty Albion's mighty king)
and Guenevere his wife had *their* wedding,

125

compared to that prepared for Gotelind.
What food! They really didn't live on wind!
And when all was prepared, young Helmbrecht sent
his messenger, as had been the intent,
who made all haste to go to Helmbrecht's farm,
and brought the sister with him on his arm.

When Filch-a-lamb got word that she had come
and Gotelind was now amongst the throng,
he rushed towards her when he saw her there,
and welcomed her in tones courtly and fair:
'Greetings, good Gotelind, most noble maid.'
'And to you, Filch-a-lamb,' the girl replied.
The couple gazed into each other's eyes
with looks of longing and with loving sighs,
he looked at her, and then she looked at him,
then they gazed at each other once again.
Sir Filch-a-lamb, with gentle loving words
very soon struck a sympathetic chord
with Gotelind, who blushed and glanced away,
and then replied in a most courtly way,
then Gotelind gazed sweetly at her swain,
while lovestruck Filch-a-lamb gazed back again.

A grey-haired elder now came to the fore,
who knew the proper form of service for
the celebration of a marriage, and
inside a circle made the couple stand.
Then first he spoke to Filch-a-lamb, and said:
'Do you take Gotelind, this lovely maid,
to be your lawful wife? Then say *I do*.'
''course I will,' said the lad. 'Too bloody true!'
He asked the young man to reply once more.
He said: 'Too right, I'll have her, that's for sure!'
He tried a third time: 'Will you say *I do*?'
The young man said: 'I keep on telling you
that by my earthly and eternal life
I'll have this woman gladly for my wife.'

The old man spoke to Gotelind instead:
'Do you, child, take Sir Filch-a-lamb' he said,
'to be your lawful husband? Say *I do*.'
'In God's name yes, if I can have him too!'
'Do you take Filch-a-lamb . . . ' once more he tried.
'Of course I do. Let's have him,' she replied.
And then a third time: 'Will you have this man?'
'With pleasure and as often as I can!'

And so he married Gotelind quickly
to Filch-a-lamb before the company,
and the young man, for the rest of his life,
was joined with Gotelind as man and wife.
The guests all sang together after this,
he raised the veil and gave the bride a kiss,
and then they sat down, every single guest
so that they could enjoy the wedding-feast.
The courtly offices were in the hands
of other members of young Helmbrecht's band.
Helmbrecht (or Gobble-goods) looked after all
the horses of the guests, as the marshal.
Eat-a-ram served the drinks, all of the best,
while Swag-bag ushered in and led the guests
to their appropriate places at the board,
both local friends, and from further abroad,
acting as seneschal. The worst of them,
Sir Rattle-safe, presided as the chamberlain,
Cow-gobbler was the master of the food,
and supervised the kitchens – all the good
roast and stewed meat came from Cow-gobbler – and
the bread was given out by Toss-Pot's hand.
This was a wedding-feast to beat the lot!
Sir Wolf-throat and his good friend, Sir Wolfsgut,
and Sir Wolf-snout as well – they came, all three,
and they all ate and drank voraciously,
downing a dozen cups of wine at least
to celebrate this splendid wedding-feast.
Before these men, food just melted away

like snowflakes on a burning summer's day,
or if some mighty storm-wind had just roared
and cleared the food right off the very board.
I know they ate up every single thing
that from the kitchens anyone could bring,
and I don't think a poor dog, passing by,
would find meat on the bones they had sucked dry.
It doesn't matter anyway, because
there is a proverb I'd remind you of:
it runs, 'eat, drink and be merry' but still
there is another sentence that I'll tell:
'eat, drink, enjoy yourself,' and here is why:
it goes on, 'for tomorrow we shall die.'
That's why there was such guzzling of drink;
'enjoy yourself, it's later than you think,'
and so it was with this whole would-be court.
It was very much later than they thought.

For suddenly fair Gotelind, the bride,
shuddered, and to her brand-new husband cried:
'Alas, a chill runs down my spine with fear,
and I feel hostile strangers coming near,
intent on doing us a deal of harm.
Father, mother, why did I leave the farm?
What prompted me this stupid thing to do,
so now I am so far away from you!
Now I'm afraid that those three sacks with all
the plunder, might lead now to my downfall
and cause me nothing but the greatest harm.
I wish that I were back home on the farm,
I wish I'd never come to be a bride,
and now I wait here simply terrified.
I didn't feast so well at father's table,
but his food is far preferable
to all the dangers I now have to face
by staying with the others in this place.
I've heard it said a thousand times or more
that if you are too greedy, then you're sure

to lose it all! We're led by greed
into the very jaws of hell indeed,
because it is a very sinful state.
Alas, I now repent, but it's too late.
Alas, I listened to my brother's words,
I wish now that I never would have heard
of Helmbrecht's plans and what he had in store;
all I can do is weep for evermore.'
The bride, Gotelind, very quickly learned
that farmer Helmbrecht's poor fare, that she'd spurned,
would after all have been better by far
than all the fine fish Filch-a-lamb gave her.
For when they all had eaten of the best,
and they had sat awhile to take their rest
and listen to the cheerful minstrelsy
(after the bride and bridegroom paid the fee)
suddenly – what a shock it must have been –
they saw the law-men come upon the scene,
five officers who would enforce the law,
the hanging judge and his assistants four.
They quickly overcame the drunken ten,
though some of them tried to run off again
and hide behind the stove, or under chairs,
and one ran here and the other ran there.
But any that escaped the men of law
was dragged out by the hair across the floor
by the hangman's assistant – this is true
as the whole tale that I am telling you.
A proper thief, however bold the man may be,
and even if he has the strength of three
still won't escape the hangman in the end,
and that indeed now happened to all ten.
They were all rounded up and quickly tied
up by the hangman and his men; they tried
to break away, but for their pains
the hangman's men soon had them clapped in chains.

Gotelind lost her lovely bridal gown,

and by a hedgerow she herself was found
in parlous state without her wedding-dress.
She had to cover up her nakedness
with hands across her breasts – the play
was over, and she'd learned the hardest way.
And what else happened to her after this?
Well, many men were there to bear witness
that God really claims vengeance when there's need,
and this tale proves that this is true indeed.

A thief may trick a hundred men or more,
but he is powerless before the law.
If our thief only sees a hangman, then
he'll pale, his eyes will dim, and once again
he'll become weak, however great his might,
defenceless when faced with the force of right,
so even a lame hangman can, at will,
take him; all his cunning, thieving skill
is useless, whatever his bold intent,
when faced with Justice and God's Punishment.

And now I'll tell about the trial, and
the condemnation of this robber band,
when they were taken for their felony
and ended up upon the gallows-tree.
Gotelind had to watch as Filch-a-lamb
had two cow-hides tied to his body, and
she saw his burden was the very least
because he'd been the bridegroom at the feast
and had less on him than the others there;
the rest had rather heavy loads to bear.
His new brother-in-law had to drag in
three whole raw cow-hides on his shoulders then;
and this was only legal and correct
for Gobble-goods, the stupid young Helmbrecht.
Each had to carry some great weight, and pile
it up as tribute when they came to trial.
But defence for them could be prepared.

If anybody thinks they should be spared,
then God should cut *his* life a little short!
(At least, that's what I think the Good Lord ought
to do.) I know the judge thought so, at least,
and he'd have treated any wild beast
with greater kindness than this wicked band
after the crimes committed by their hands.

The executioner hanged nine of them that night,
but one he left alive – it was his right
of tithing – one in ten he could elect
to save – and that was Gobble-goods Helmbrecht.

Well, what must be, must be – that's what they say
and the Lord God will never look away
and take no notice of a wicked crime –
that much is clear from Helmbrecht's fate this time:
they now took vengeance for his father, when
his eyes were put out by the hangman's men;
but even that was not redress enough –
they now avenged his mother, and cut off
one of his hands and one of his feet, too,
in vengeance for the insult that he threw
as greeting to his parents when he came
to see them – bringing only pain and shame.
He did not greet with courtesy; instead
'you grubby little peasant' he had said,
then called his mother 'common little wife.'
Because of these sins, Helmbrecht's wretched life
was made a thousand times worse – every breath
he drew just made him wish for death
rather than live like this, in all his shame,
spared by the hangman for a life of pain.

Helmbrecht the robber, crippled, maimed and blind
now took leave of his sister Gotelind
at a crossroads, beneath the gallows-tree
and he set off in pain and misery.

Young Helmbrecht the blind thief of course now had
to walk on crutches, led by a small lad,
and he came to his father's farm once more;
but this time he was driven from their door.
However pitiful the young man looked today,
listen to what his father had to say!

'*Deu sal*, Sir Beggar-man! I well recall
when I once served in our overlord's hall
(albeit it was many years ago)
that that's a proper greeting – that I know!
But on your way, you grubby blind beggar.
I know that you have everything and more
than any courtier could ever want or need –
some foreigner will take you in, indeed,
so all you'll get from me is a good-day,
that's what blind robbers deserve, anyway.
Why should I waste any more words on you,
you blinded robber? What am I to do?
Make sure you very quickly get away
– and I'll not brook even a small delay
before I set my groom upon you, too,
and make sure that he beats you black and blue,
like no blind man was ever hurt before –
You may be blind, but your hide would be sore!
In any case, I'd reckon it a waste
if I should give you any food to taste.
So clear off out of here and leave my door,
and never ever come back any more.'

'No, sir, I beg you, let me stay with you,'
said the blind man, 'and then I'll tell you true
what I am known as here in all the land,
in God's name recognise me, who I am!'
The father said: 'Well, make it quick, and then
you can be off and on your way again.
It's late, someone may take you in somewhere,
but from me you'll get nothing, that I swear.'

In tones of agony and bitter shame
the young man gave his father his true name
and said: 'Sir, recognise me, I'm your son.'

'Well, did they put the eyes out of the one
who gave himself the name of Gobble-goods,
and had no fear that any hangman could
ever catch him – and if pursued by three
he'd still escape them very easily?
Oh yes, you said that iron bars you'd bite
when you rode off upon a horse that night
that I'd sold cattle, cloth and corn to buy!
And now a blinded beggar hobbles by!
It makes me angry when I think of all
the good things that I sold to no avail,
when I have always worked to get my bread.
So even if you lay there nearly dead
of hunger, you would never get a crust.
Now shift yourself – I'm telling you, you must
clear off, get out, keep moving, do not slack,
and what's more, make sure you never come back.'
The blind man heard all this, and then he said:
'If you won't have me as your son, instead
in God's name and the name of charity
please look into your heart and pity me
as any blind beggar, and let me come
into your house just for a little time
and give a poor sick man some charity
out of your Christian love and piety.
The countrymen all hate me everywhere,
and now, alas, you also hate me here.
Alas, I cannot live another day
if from your door you will drive me away.'
The old man laughed and mocked the beggar too,
although his heart was breaking – for he knew
this was his flesh and blood, one of his kin,
although he stood there blinded before him.
He said: 'You rampaged wildly through the land,

your horse raged onwards and you never reined,
you galloped and you trampled people down,
their sufferings never caused you to frown.
Your robbing and your thieving was so bad
that you stole every single thing they had
from many of the farmers' families.
Do you remember, though, I once had three
prophetic dreams? Now of these the first two
have very clearly both proved to be true.
But if my third dream (and the worst of all)
should happen – much worse will befall!
So get away from here, and rapidly,
before that dream becomes reality,
and you must suffer much more than before.
Groom, go and put the bars on all the doors,
tonight I want to rest well in my bed.
I'd rather feed, from now until I'm dead,
some fellow that I've not set eyes upon,
than give a crust to you! And now, begone.'
And thus every debt was paid off fully
on this blind criminal, who seemed to be
a figure from some nightmare, full of doom.
'Get rid of him,' he now said to the groom,
'get him out of my sight for evermore.'
He slapped the lad who led Helmbrecht. 'Be sure
that your fine master would merit the same,
only to hit a blind man would be shame,
so I must satisfy myself with you.
I still have enough breeding that I do
avoid some things, and my restraint is strong,
but be warned, that may change before too long.
So be off, wretched scoundrel, wicked man,
get out as quickly as you ever can,
Your very presence fills me with disgust.'
And yet the mother did give him a crust
into his hand, as if she'd fed a child.
The blinded thief who'd been Helmbrecht the wild
set off across the fields, and everywhere

he went the farmers shouted to him there:
'Hey, robber Helmbrecht, hear what I've to say!
If on the farm you had chosen to stay,
working the land and ploughing, same as me,
a blinded cripple you would not now be!'

And thus he suffered while one year went past
till death by hanging brought an end at last.
Now I shall tell you how this came to be.
A farmer saw him once by chance when he
was one day walking through the forest, to collect
some firewood, and then he spotted Helmbrecht
(quite early in the morning); and he saw
the man who'd robbed him of his cow before
–a valuable one, it had cost him dear.
So when he saw blind Helmbrecht come so near
he called his people to him, and he asked
if they would come and help him in his task.
'Gladly,' said one of them – 'I'll gladly do
whatever you want, beat him black and blue,
I'll happily grind him into the ground,
if no-one holds me back, now that I've found
the one who robbed me and who robbed my wife,
who took our goods and ruined us for life,
who stole the very garments off our back!
I've got the right to get revenge for that.'
Another who was there said: 'Wait for me,
for even if he had the strength of three
I'd kill him with these two bare hands of mine,
the filthy wretch, the villain and the swine,
he broke into my stores and stole the lot,
robbed us of every single thing we'd got.'
The next man who had come along there said,
trembling with inner anger as he did
so: 'I shall kill him like a very rat,
and I too have every right to do that.
He came along one night a while back
and took my child, and threw him in a sack,

when we inside the house were all asleep.
We woke up when the child began to weep
and scream and cry to us for help; but no –
Helmbrecht just laughed, and threw it in the snow.
My child without doubt would then have died
if I had not come quickly to his side.'
A fifth man said: 'It really pleases me
that Helmbrecht's within reach of us, I see,
so I can take revenge on him as well
and help to send this wretched man to hell.
He raped my daughter when to us he came,
so I don't care if he *is* blind or lame,
I'll see him hanging from the nearest tree;
that time he nearly put an end to me,
and I only just managed to escape.
If he were twice as tall and twice as great
I'd get revenge on him, the evil wretch,
and penetrate the deepest wood to fetch
him out – let's go and get him if we can.'
'Get him,' they all cried out, and to a man
ran after Helmbrecht, rushing to make sure
that he did not escape them any more,
and while they rained blows on him, they all said:
'Helmbrecht, that cape you've got upon your head
is something the hangman forgot to take!'
He had indeed. But now the famous cape
was utterly destroyed, torn up and lost,
no matter what had been its one-time cost.
We started with the cape – let's end with it;
there wasn't left a single little bit
that was more than a centimetre wide –
the parrots and the larks, and all beside,
the hawks and turtle-doves so very fine
that had embellished Helmbrecht's hood – this time
they all were scattered, thrown upon the ground,
and little scraps of it lay all around,
not only hood, but also Helmbrecht's hair!
I've told the story and I've told it fair,

so now you must believe me when I say
what happened to the hood that dreadful day,
and how they ripped it into bits so small
and tore his hair out so that he was bald,
without a single lock upon his head
of that long flaxen hair. But now instead
he was shorn of it, all his joy and pride
lay scattered all around on the roadside.
But there was worse to come for Helmbrecht there:
they grabbed the blind thief, made him say his prayers,
and when he'd done, they took a clump of earth,
and gave it to the sinner; all its worth
was as a token that might serve him well
when he set out upon the road to hell.
And then they hanged him on the highest tree.
His father's dream – the last one of the three –
was thus proved true when he was hanged that way.
And of Helmbrecht, that's all there is to say.

Youth can be arrogant, and find absurd
their mother's and their father's warning words,
so let such youth be warned by me today
not to behave like Helmbrecht anyway.
For if they do, I know that I can state
they will be caught, and they'll share Helmbrecht's fate.
Helmbrecht had made the streets unsafe for men;
he died, and now they are safe once again,
with Helmbrecht safely hanging from a tree.
So listen, youth, and listen carefully:
Think very hard indeed – that is my rule
before dismissing me as just a fool;
fools and wise men can both give you wise words.
So what if Helmbrecht, whose tale we have heard,
should spawn some imitators, copy-cats?
They would be little Helmbrechts, and for that
the world would have no peace till it could see
them make the same way to the gallows-tree.

If you should read this story, pray for me
that God upon my soul should have mercy,
and smile upon a poet, poor in fame:
Wernher der Gartenaere is my name.

The Wandering Scholars

The best-known of the medieval wandering scholars, the secular Latin poet known just as the 'Archpoet' died in about 1165, and seems to have been a German attached to the retinue of Reinald, chancellor to Frederick Barbarossa. These wandering poets tended to stick to wine, women, song and gambling as their themes, alternating with requests to their patrons for funds. The Archpoet's *Confession* is very well-known, but rather long, so this is an extract. The last strophe here has been called 'the greatest drinking song ever.'

The Archpoet

The Confession

There's a burning in my guts,
with rage the fires play;
now from my inner bitterness
hear what I've got to say.
I'm made of insubstantial stuff
and less than nothing weigh,
I'm no more than a fallen leaf
the winds can blow away.

Now, this is what wise men are like:
their natural property
is to be anchored to a rock,
and settled solidly.
I, therefore, have to be a fool,
a flowing stream, that's me!
Never beneath the same sky twice
and always floating free.

I'm drifting on the sea of life,
a ship without a crew,
just like the free birds of the air,

139

high-flying in the blue.
No chains can ever bind me down,
no locks hold me – it's true!
I go and find a few like minds,
debauchers through and through.

To me a solemn attitude
is just an imposition;
I find a life of jollity
a sweeter proposition;
pursuing the delights of love
is my preferred condition,
and Venus never works on men
of pompous disposition.

I'm off along the broadest path
while I'm still young and vernal;
I'll get involved with lots of vice
and the virtues I'll spurn all.
I'm hungrier for earthly lusts
than for the life eternal,
and since the spirit's a dead loss,
I'll focus on the carnal.

I'm sure that you will be discreet
and hope you will be fair;
however – what a way to die!
Such sweet poison I'll dare.
You see, I'm pierced right to the heart
by beauty rich and rare,
and even though I may not touch,
my mind is right in there!

It's hard to keep your urges down,
restrain your manly vigour.
No man can keep his thoughts all pure
faced with a shapely figure!
We're far too young to be confined

by morals and their rigour;
our bodies want to take control,
the pressures just get bigger.

. . .

The second thing they throw at me
is that I like a flutter.
Well, now and then I've lost my shirt,
and frozen in some gutter.
But who cares if the body's cold,
the mind loses its clutter,
it gives an edge to all the songs
and verses that I utter.

My drinking is another thing
that they're always decrying.
I've never scorned the habit yet,
and I shall *not* be trying.
At least, not till my eyes make out
the angels to me flying,
their choirs to me singing a
requiem for the dying.

To snuff it in the boozer, boys,
has always been my plan.
It's so that I can fade and die
with a bottle in my hand.
Then all the angel choirs will sing
as merrily as they can:
'May the good Lord be merciful
towards this drinking man!'

Cecco Angiolieri

Cecco Angiolieri of Siena (ca 1260–ca 1312/3) has actually been described as a 'raucous beatnik.' Certainly his very forceful poems (of which these are probably the best known) celebrate indulgence in drinking, sex and gambling, just like those of the Archpoet. But Cecco's are coupled with a hatred of his parents: of his father for being rich but miserly, and of his mother just because she hated *him*. He didn't get on too well with his wife, either, nor was he keen on Dante, whom he attacked in two sonnets. These, however, are more general.

Cecco Agniolieri of Siena

Two Sonnets

If I were fire, I'd burn up everything;
if I were wind, I'd tempest it away;
if I were water, drown it in a day;
if I were God, to hell the world I'd fling;
if I were Pope, now *that* would make me sing!
I'd take the loot and make the Christians pay!
If I were Emperor – hear what I say! –
I'd chop their heads off, commoner or king!

If I were death, I'd call my father's name;
if I were life I'd run from him again,
and for my mother I'd do just the same!
If I were Cecco (as I am), well, then
I'd roger every young and bouncy dame
and leave the fat old slags to other men.

There are three boons and blessings known to men,
but, sadly, I don't often get a share.
Women, the boozer and the gambling den –
those are the things that really make me cheer.
But I can only get them now and then,
because my purse won't let me. It's unfair!
and when I think of it, I howl with pain,
that lack of money makes my pleasures rare.

So, dammit, let him get it with a spear!
Papa, that's who! His great allowance-freeze
means that I'd come back broke from France, I fear!
You'd prize cash out of him with far *less* ease
(even at Easter, gift-time of the year)
than catch a tiger with mouse-trap and cheese.

The Destruction of the World

The Reformation brought a certain amount of mud-slinging with it, and a Swiss Protestant, Jacob Ruf (whose surname is spelt in more ways than one would believe possible for a monosyllable, and who doubled as surgeon-obstetrician for the town of Zurich and religious dramatist) compares the Bible story of the 'wicked generation' that God wiped out in the flood, with current (he implies 'Catholic') society, in which people fail to listen to Luther just as they failed to listen to Noah in the old days. First of all we are shown the sons of Seth in the city of Hanoch eyeing up (against God's commandment) the wicked daughters of Cain, a predatory bunch against whom the Sethites don't stand a chance. Then we see their descendants; but it is a very modern-looking society in what is obviously meant to be sixteenth-century Rome rather than the ancient world that is drowned in Ruf's climax to his two-day outdoor spectacular, first performed in 1555. The only ones who are worried are the city Guards. But Guards in Rome in the 1550s were Ruf's fellow-countrymen, the Swiss, just like today.

Jacob Ruf

Adam and Eve

[*The start of the wicked generation: the sons of Seth lust after the daughters of Cain – and vice versa (Act V, lines 4615–4766)*]

FIRST SETHITE MAN
(or son of the race of God's children)
  Hallo, old friend! God's blessing, too!
SECOND SETHITE MAN
  My thanks! Now what, my friend, of you?
  What have you done? Where have you been?
  Tell me about the things you've seen.

FIRST SETHITE MAN
>I've been in Hanoch, visiting.

SECOND SETHITE MAN
>>What news from there? What's happening?
>>Tell me, I'm curious to hear
>>if you've seen something strange or rare.

FIRST SETHITE MAN
>>I've never, in all my born days,
>>seen folk more beautiful than those
>>in Hanoch, in the Cainite town.
>>The women are of great renown,
>>shapely, well-dressed, clean and neat,
>>and flocks of them in every street!
>>You won't see better anywhere!
>>And anyone who turns up there,
>>regardless where he comes from, he
>>will be received most civilly.
>>They're well brought up in every way,
>>they sing, they dance, and they can play
>>the fiddle, organ, flute and fife.
>>I've not seen finer in my life.
>>If it were not tabu, I'd say
>>I'd marry one of them today.

SECOND SETHITE MAN
>>Odds fish! What's this you're telling me?
>>We're God's folk, we're Seth's family,
>>and God forbade us, as His men,
>>to have dealings with Cain's children
>>of any sort. And so, what's more,
>>did Adam, our progenitor,
>>(whom we buried not long ago),
>>*and* Enoch, whom God took up, too –
>>he warned against the kin of Cain,
>>so you should really think again.
>>With that lot we must not mix in –
>>you'd only fall into great sin,
>>you really ought to keep away.

145

FIRST SETHITE MAN

       God help us! What things you *do* say!
       What would it hurt, if I should dare
       to find myself a wife down there
       in Hanoch, pretty, just my size
       (yours too – you want to trust your eyes!)
       and if we have a kid or two
       then they'd serve God, like me and you.
       If I bring her to *my* belief
       wouldn't that be a great relief?

FIRST SETHITE MAN

       No, no, my friend, that's wrong, I fear!
       God's commandment was very clear:
       Cain's lot are unbelievers, so
       to them we really must not go
       for wives (or *any* other plans!)
       That's why I say 'no' out of hand.
       And you, my friend, would God's law break
       if you an unbeliever take.

FIRST SETHITE MAN

       If you'd look for yourself, my friend,
       you'd say there's no sin, in the end!
       If you should see this lovely lot,
       you'd say they're better than we've got!
       I don't think that it's sinfulness
       for me to take a wife, I guess,
       who'd love me, and who's sweet and fine,
       and whose desires match up with mine.
       I'd live for her and she for me –
       I wish, my friend, that you'd agree!
       I'm sure of her God would approve,
       more than a wife who did not love
       me anyway, and I could find
       no love for her of any kind.
       Is that God's holy marriage law?
       No happiness is there, I'm sure!
       I'll take what wife I want, and you
       cannot dissuade me from that view!

SECOND SETHITE MAN
>It's up to you, dear friend, although
>God has commanded us, you know,
>to lust after a girl is sin,
>nor may we mingle with Cain's kin,
>because they're full of fleshly lust
>and proud and haughty, and we must
>avoid them, everyone the same,
>for they are full of sin and shame,
>pride, envy, greed – all of that race,
>so God has turned from them His face.
>There's no good in that common herd,
>who twist and who reject God's word,
>who distort all propriety,
>and only live in luxury.
>So friend, if for a wife you'd care,
>make sure you do not seek one there.
>Beautiful girls are close at hand,
>so why not take from *our* land?

FIRST SETHITE MAN
>You won't dissuade me now, dear man,
>I'll take the prettiest I can
>in any country that I know –
>and I shan't be ashamed to go.

SECOND SETHITE MAN
>On your head be it – in God's name,
>go forth and walk right into shame,
>that tribe lives shockingly, I say,
>and God may someday make you pay.

[*The first man leaves to find the Cainite women*]

***

FIRST CAINITE WOMAN
(or daughter of the race of the children of men)
>Good day to you, my cousin! Say,
>where are you heading this fine day?
>For by the way you're dressed I see

147

that you're out walking purposefully!

SECOND CAINITE WOMAN

Well, thank you, cousin! You are kind.
Yes, I *do* have something in mind.

FIRST CAINITE WOMAN

You're lively! Tell me if you can!

SECOND CAINITE WOMAN

Odd's lungs! What I want is a man
from God's folk! I've heard people say
they're now like us in every way,
they're good-looking and cheerful men,
love women and are good to them
and kind – I need that sort of man
so I'll do everything I can
and try and see if I can catch
a Sethite man to make a match.

FIRST CAINITE WOMAN

Odd's bodikins! You are a clot!
You want a man from God's own lot?
I think you've gone a bit too far.
Don't you know what their customs are?
For life and lust they just don't care,
they're always on their knees in prayer,
they don't go in for women, so
these things are what you ought to know!
Besides, the main thing that I meant
is: their *religion's* different.

SECOND CAINITE WOMAN

So their religion's not the same?
That's nothing to do with the game.
And any man I'm sure I'll twist
to be *my* co-religionist!
Come on, women have tricks, we can
soon get our way with any man,
we'll use attractions, swiftly done,
you'll see! So all I need is one,
and he'll soon see who's in the right,
in daylight or in bed at night.

I'll get him with my woman's wiles,
if I have to chase a hundred miles!

FIRST CAINITE WOMAN

Odds gherkins, cousin! I can tell
you're barmy, and you're deaf as well,
to go and try and find a man
foolishly in a foreign land
amongst God's people! What you say!
They've no lusts of the flesh, and they
just don't *enjoy* things, that's no good.

SECOND CAINITE WOMAN

Come on! they're only flesh and blood,
they're born and made the selfsame way
as we are, and that's why I say
not one of them is quite *that* pious
that when I offer, he won't try us.
Besides, they're gentlemen, you see,
so they'll be very nice to me.
That's why I'm off into that land
to try and catch myself a man . . .

[*Later, Noah tries to warn the descendants of this union that the
flood is coming; but they are carousing, and nobody, from the local
count to the kitchenboy, takes much notice*]

NOAH

God's greeting to you, my dear friends,
but when will you all turn from sin,
stop shaming God with blasphemy?
This must lead to catastrophe!
God's judgement has been passed on you
and soon you'll see what he can do
for punishment – of that be sure!

MASTER OF CEREMONIES

Oh, shut your trap and say no more,
stop blethering, and make an end,
that's my advice to you, my friend,
and leave us to our food and drinks.
How can *you* tell us what God thinks?

149

You just accuse us constantly
of sin – including the gentry!
You won't give up or go away.
Be warned – sometime you'll have to pay.

NOAH

The rage of God, the Trinity,
is threefold over you – really –
according to His holy name.
Through Him the world at first became
created, formed out of the void,
and now it all can be destroyed,
wiped out, demolished completely –
that's what God has revealed to me.
So you should do your best again,
repent and turn away from sin.

CHAMBERLAIN

Don't threaten us, that's what I say,
and that's enough of 'judgement day,'
clear off, that's the advice I give –
you're far too argumentative,
but won't persuade us, that's for sure.
We'll go on and we'll hate you more.

NOAH

You really do not understand!
God wants to flood all of the land
with everything that's on the earth
that He created, brought to birth.
God sent me to you to dissuade
away from sin the things He'd made.

THE COUNT

If God intends to drown the lot,
then that includes you, does it not?
In God Himself I'll trust instead
that things won't happen as you've said.
Have you ever seen God lay low
His handiwork? Or do you know
His mind? Have you visited God,
that you're so certain of His word?

You talk about it as if *you*
were telling *God* what He should do,
making Him follow your advice
to do your bidding in a trice!
God hasn't given up His throne!
So we'll enjoy ourselves! Begone!

MAYOR

If you just want to make a fuss,
cause trouble and just bother us,
you might as well shut up! And so
we really think you ought to go.

NOAH

My God! My God! Why be that way?
You should be pleased at what I say,
that God gives you a warning true
and sends His mercy down to you.
But warnings aren't the slightest use
if you continue to abuse
yourselves with all these acts of lust,
for God will punish, as He must!
Your lordship, sirs, dear friends, resist!
Repent, and from your sins desist.

FIRST SERVANT

Old man, for all your gloomy chat
judgement won't come as fast as that!
You only want to spoil our fun,
wreck the party for everyone.
You should have stayed at home instead
and had some fun yourself in bed!
Just leave the gentry and us all
in peace, so we can have a ball!

SECOND SERVANT

Noah, Noah, please hear my plea,
just go away, and rapidly.
I tell you this, and it is true,
there's really nothing here for you!
Before too long the master will
call for his wine – they'll drink their fill

151

and when they're full they'll break your head,
so you'd best get away instead.

NOAH

It really makes me very sad
that your reaction is so bad,
that you will not heed God's intent
for judgement and for punishment.
You sin and sin, and never fear,
God's warnings you just *will* not hear.
Instead you scorn the holy name
and live a wicked life of shame
with whoring, drinking, lust and pride
behind closed doors – yes *and* outside! –
without honour and decency.
You only care for luxury.
God will not suffer this much more.
One day He'll be avenged, for sure.
[. . .]

COOK

I beg you, sing another song,
or you'll get beaten before long.
No-one believes you anyway.

DRUMMER

Perhaps I'll help him on his way.
Why should we listen to his words?
He's really not that close to God,
and if God did punish us all
it wouldn't help old Noah at all,
'cause he'd be drowned too anyhow.
He can't get over that one, now.

KITCHENBOY

Clear off, old man, I'm telling you
if not, we'll beat you black and blue.
You'd better stop your drivelling noise –
I'll have to thump you otherwise.

NOAH

God's mercy on your spirits poor,
you won't hear warnings any more,

152

whatever I may cry or shout.
Well, you will very soon find out
about God's vengeance and His rage
on you, this sybaritic age,
blasphemers, cursers, evil race
which simply will not seek God's grace
or change its lifestyle any more.
And all God's warnings you ignore.
Your hearts have sunk too deeply in
your decadence and vice and sin.
You've all made your deliberate choice,
agreeing, as if with one voice,
to love the way the devil shows.
You'll have to pay for it, you know,
this very day. The hour of pain!
I've told you time and time again,
but now no more – I've said my word –
and now it's in the hands of God.
Perhaps He'll change your minds today
to live your lives the proper way,
and maybe show His mercy too,
and moderate His doom on you.

COUNT

Just get yourself from here, and quick,
or else you're sure to get a kick.
You think your prophecies of doom
and ravings full of direst gloom
might even make God turn about
and force God's hand to carry out
what *you* want – God would work for you,
not for Himself! It will not do!
Will you not grasp? We don't believe
your stuff, and so you've got to leave.
Get out of here – you'd better run
the rest of us want wine and fun!

NOAH

God won't pardon your attitude,
your arrogance and all your crude

153

behaviour. And on this very day
you'll have a different bill to pay.
Just wait – only an hour or two –
the wrath of God will come to you!

[*The play ends with the ultimate act of social cleansing for a
decadent society, as the court is drowned in mid-party. In that Bible-
conscious age, though, one wonders whether anyone remembered that
the first scene involving drunkenness in the Bible comes after the
flood and involves none other than Noah himself?*]

SEX

Courtly love is one of the phenomena that everyone associates with the Middle Ages, but even though it is predicated upon an adultery (in theory, at least), it is not necessarily wicked. If you have marriages arranged without love, then you are bound to get a reaction that is equal and opposite. In any case, the literary expression of courtly love was highly conventional, and sometimes so formalised that the pedestal upon which the adored lady was placed was so high that you wouldn't have been able to see her even if she had really existed in the first place, which often she didn't. Nor, really, is there genuine evil in all the one-off adulterers and cuckolded husbands in the comic tales, the *fabliaux*. Misuse or abuse of power is definitely a sign of decadence, however, be it regal or religious, and so is glorying in excess. 'Brazening it out' is also wicked, as in the very early version, given here, of the snow-baby story.

The tale of the snow-baby is one of the most familiar in the Middle Ages. The anecdote of the woman's attempt to explain away a supernumerary child acquired while her husband was away on a protracted business trip, and of his subsequent revenge, is told concisely in a Latin poem from the so-called *Cambridge Songs*; one of the earliest versions (eleventh century), it is probably also the best. The manuscript is in Cambridge now, but was copied in Canterbury from a Rhineland original, and the copyist managed to insert a quite extraneous stanza into our poem. Here the characters are Swabian, from Constance; but the balance is perfect between the woman's tale of Alpine thirst and the husband's counter-tale of the burning sun.

The Cambridge Songs

The Snow-Baby

Come gather round, people,
and you'll hear a story,
a jolly tale that I've to tell,
how a woman once cheated
her Swabian husband
who cheated her back just as well.

The Swabian came from
the city of Constance,
but went overseas all the time
(in import-and-export);
his wife was a sex-pot
whom he left (far too often) behind.

Hardly had he
dipped an oar
into the sea
when suddenly
a storm-wind rose,
the tempest roared
the waters raged
and much, much more,
until the weary
traveller
made landfall on
a distant shore.

Meanwhile at home
his wife refused
to sit and brood.
Actors dropped in,
and all the clan
helped her forget
her absent man.

One night after
a party, she
got pregnant and
gave birth (improperly)
within the proper time.

Two years having
gone, our weary
traveller returned
with joy.
Found his faithless
wife awaiting
carrying a little boy.
They embraced and
then he asked her
where she'd got the lad.
He said:
'Come my dear, you'd
better tell me,
else I shall knock off your head.'

Very fearful
of her husband,
she resorted to
a lie.
'Husband dear,'
she said, 'dear husband,
once, up in the Alps, on high,
I was trapped and
very thirsty,
slaked my thirst with snow, and I
found that it had made me pregnant,
so I bore this wretched boy!'

When five years had passed,
the merchant
thought he'd take
another trip.

Got it all prepared and took the
snow-child with him
on his ship.

In the southern seas
arriving,
he brought out
the lad, and sold
him to an Arab for a hundred
pounds, and came home
with the gold.

He went
to his house and
he said
to his wife:
'For sorrow you must be prepared.
For the child is lost
that you so much loved,
and for which I, like you
greatly cared.

For a
tempest rose up
and tossed
us in its rage,
till there on a sandbank we lay.
The hot sun beat down,
and tormented us all,
but the snow-baby
melted away.'

That's how the husband
defeated the lady,
out-cheated the cheater
and won.
For the child born of snow
of course had to go,

and was melted away by
the sun.

Marie de France

Lady Mary from France composed her poetry at the court of the Norman kings (to whom she may have been related) in London in the last part of the twelfth century. She wrote a number of *lais*, verse narratives for which she usually claimed Celtic origin, and in this one the scenario is old. Admittedly the best-known abuser of royal power – King David – actually got away with it, or at least got off with a caution from Nathan, but here there is a savage twist to the bath motif. This is not conventionalised dalliance. It is abuse of power, and the vengeance is justified.

Marie de France

The Tale of King Equitan

How many noble lords once dwelt
in Brittany! The Bretons felt
in former times that it would be
a benefit and courtesy
that famous deeds be kept in mind
–the deeds of men of every kind –
so they composed their rhyming lays
to give these tales to later days,
and of these pieces, I recall
one that was unforgettable,
about King Equitan, ruler
of Nantes, a chivalrous *seigneur*.

King Equitan was noble, and
much loved throughout his own homelands,
fond, too, of amorous delights,
a worthy and a courteous knight.
Now: life's a wasteland, that's for sure,
if you've no interest in *l'amour*.
Here's what love is: when in its sway,

160

you can't think in a rational way.

Equitan had a seneschal,
a knight unfailingly loyal,
administrator of his land,
who ruled for him with even hand,
because (except when fighting wars
or following some urgent cause)
the king would never put aside
his pleasures – to the hunt he'd ride.

The seneschal was married, and
his wife would suffer in that land,
but she was beautiful, and she
was of well-bred gentility;
her form was shapely, and her face
was filled by nature with pure grace;
her eyes were grey, her features shone –
a mouth like none had looked upon! –
no-one could match her in those days!

The king had often heard her praised,
and used to greet her courteously,
and send her presents privately;
he pined for her, and often would
sit and talk with her, if he could.

For hunting and for private sport
the king would go far from the court,
and once he lodged in the castle
owned by his worthy seneschal,
when he returned from hunting deer.
The lady – she was living there.

The king could now converse with her
at length, show what his feelings were.
He found her courteous and wise,
lovely in body, face and eyes,

161

and well-disposed and debonnaire.
Love had the king well in her snare!
Cupid had fired the fatal dart,
wounded the king right to the heart,
and left him vanquished on the field.
Now thought and reason had to yield.
He took the lady by surprise,
and made her pensive. With sad sighs
she listened to his love intense,
and she could put up no defence.

The king got no repose that night,
but blamed himself for this new plight
and said: 'Alas, what destiny
has brought me here to this country?
Seeing this lady once again
has been the cause of so much pain
that all my body trembles so.
I think that she must love me, though,
but if I love her, on my life
I sin – she is my bondsman's wife.
With him my faith and honesty
must rest – and likewise his with me.
If he by some chance should find out
then it would grieve him, without doubt.

However, would it not be worse
if he deflect me from my course?
This lady needs to love someone,
or have a lover. What will come
of all her beauty if she can
not take a lover? Any man
under the vault of heaven would
through love of her, aspire to good!
From what I hear, the seneschal
should cause no problem here at all.
If he can't guard her properly
then he shall share his wife with me!'

The king sighed loudly and, this said,
he lay back thinking on his bed,
and then, after a while, said: 'Why
should I be suffering, when I
have no idea if she will take
me for her lover? But I'll make
a move to find out rapidly.
If she *does* feel the same, for me
the sorrow will be past and gone.
My God, but this long night drags on!
I get no rest, I toss in pain,
how many hours since darkness came!'

The king watched all the night away
in sorrow, till the break of day.
He rose, and rode out normally
but soon returned. He said that he
was sad and was oppressed by gloom
and so withdrew into his room.
The seneschal was wondering
what sadness might afflict his king
so greatly. But he could not guess
that his wife caused the king's distress.

The king, for comfort, very soon
summoned the lady to his room
and poured his heart out to her there,
saying he'd die for love of her.
She could restore his life and breath,
or she could drive him to his death.

'Lord King,' the lady answered him,
'you must allow a little time,
for now, when I am faced with you
I've no idea what I should do.
You are king, of noble line.
I am not rich enough, or fine,
for you not to choose someone higher

for your love, or for your desire.
If once you had your will of me,
I know, and know it certainly,
my lord, that you would leave me. Then
sorrow is all I'd have, and pain.
If I should take this love from you,
submit just as you wish me to,
then it would be unfair to me –
I'd bear my share unequally.
You are a king, strong in command,
my husband is your vassal, and
you think this power should confer
rights to my love, as a seigneur.
But love unequal is no love;
a poor, but loyal knight may prove
a better man, if he is just,
and worthier of love and trust
than any king or prince may be,
if he is without loyalty.
If someone loves above his state,
more highly than his wealth would rate,
he'll be in anguish day and night.
A rich man thinks he has the right
to keep a lover as his own,
by virtue of his rank alone.'

King Equitan said right away:
'Lady, enough. No more, I say.
This is not talk worthy of you,
but haggling, like a merchant, who,
in his concern for wealth and fee,
sells goods of shoddy quality.
No lady anywhere, if she
be wise and full of courtesy,
and holds love worthy of her kind,
and is not fickle in her mind,
though poor, would fail to be worth
that any great prince here on earth

should come and woo her honestly,
and serve her well, and loyally.
Those who are fickle in their hearts,
and who deceive, try to outsmart
their lovers – *they're* the cheated ones!
How many times has this been done –
it's not surprising if a man
is rightly paid back for such plans.
Most dear lady, I beg of you
to see me as your lover true,
not as your king. I am your man.
In loyalty I swear I can
do all you ask of me, and I
will do it! Help me, or I die!
You shall be mistress, I the slave,
you proud, whilst I your mercy crave.'

The king pleaded with her, and he
begged mercy of her constantly
until she gave her love in full –
he had her heart and body too.
They pledged their trust; with hand to hand
they swore love to each other, and
in that way they both kept this faith.

One day it led them to their death.

Their love endured a long time then,
but hidden from the eyes of men.
When they would meet together, they
would do it covertly, this way:
the king spoke to his men, and said
that he was going to be bled.
The doors were closed behind him there.
There was no courtier who would dare
be bold enough to venture in,
unless commanded by the king.

165

The seneschal sat in the court,
and judged cases of every sort.
The king cherished his lover, and
would have no other in that land,
nor would he marry. The idea
could not be voiced when he might hear.
His subjects, though, took that amiss.

His mistress came to hear of this
and found it greatly troubling,
and feared that she would lose the king.

When next to speak she saw her chance,
and he came seeking dalliance,
to hug and kiss and hold her tight,
and lie with her throughout the night,
she wept and sighed and showed her pain.
The king tried to calm her again
and find the cause of all her tears.
The lady told him of her fears:
'My lord, it's for our love I cry,
which robs me of my every joy.
You'll take a wife, wed some princess,
and then you'll leave me in distress.
I've heard it all. I know it's true.
But what is there for me to do?
For love of you I'll pine away
and die – there is no other way.'

The king was filled with love, and said:
'My dearest one, don't be afraid!
I've no desire to take a wife,
nor shall I leave you all my life.
Know and believe these words, my dear:
if your husband were no more here,
I'd make you queen without delay.
No man should then stand in my way.'

The lady thanked him lovingly,
and said it pleased her mightily
to hear of this, and to believe
that her love he would never leave.
But then she gave the king her word
that death *would* soon come to her lord;
she would arrange things with all speed,
if he would help her at her need.
The king agreed that he would do
whatever she would ask him to,
if good or evil were his task,
he would do everything she'd ask.

'Lord King,' she said, 'first you should
go hunting in the leafy woods
near that land where I live. And then
stay in my lord's castle again,
and there arrange that you'll be bled.
The third day after that,' she said,
'you'll bathe. Let my lord bathe there, too,
after he has been bled with you.
Tell him he must, insist firmly
that he should keep you company.
I'll have the water heated through
and tubs brought in for each of you.
His tub will be so scalding that
no man on earth could suffer it –
in it he will be burned alive,
scalded to death. He'll not survive.
When he is scalded to his doom
summon your men into the room
and his, and when they are inside
tell them their lord suddenly died.'
The king at once agreed that he
would do her bidding willingly.

Just three months passed. And then the king
went to that land to go hunting.

But he had himself bled as well,
for health, as did the seneschal.
On the third day the king decreed
that he would bathe. His host agreed.
'You'll bathe with me, sir seneschal?'
His host then answered: 'Sir, I will.'
The lady had the water boiled,
the tubs were brought when they were filled,
and each was placed before a bed.
The tub of scalding water stood
by the seneschal's bed. The good
man rose, and left the chamber where
the king was, just to get some air.
The lady came in to the king,
sat on the other bed, near him.
Soon on her husband's bed they lay
entwined, and they began to play
and to enjoy their close embrace
near where the scalding tub was placed.
They set a maid to act as ward
to watch the door, and to keep guard.

The seneschal returned too soon,
pushed at the door, but found the room
was barred against him. Angrily
he broke it down and forced entry.
He saw his lady and the king
still passionately embracing.
The king saw him, and quickly tried
his wickedness and guilt to hide,
so, naked and unthinkingly
he leapt into the tub that she
had placed there ready by the bed.

Scalded, the king at once was dead.
His evil-doing was repaid,
the would-be victim had been saved.

The seneschal was well aware
of what the king was doing there,
and so he threw his wife, head-down
into the tub, to burn and drown.
And thus they met their ends: the king,
and then the lady after him.
To any who have ears to hear
the moral is completely clear.
Plots against others will revert,
and cause the plotters to be hurt,
as in the tale I've told you now.

The Bretons made a *lai* of how
King Equitan perished and fell,
with the lady he loved so well.

Giovanni Boccaccio's *Decameron*

Boccaccio was born in 1313 (illegitimately) in France, and was brought to Florence as a child. Sent to Naples to learn finance, he discovered that he preferred literature to business studies, and became a writer. Much of his work was inspired by his love for Maria d'Aquino – 'Fiammetta' – who died in 1348, but he is best known for the massive collection of tales called the *Decameron* – ten times ten stories told by a group of ten escaping from the plague, the Black Death, in Florence. The Italian text of this story is easy to find, because for years even in English translations this one was always retained in the decent obscurity of Italian, making it handy, perhaps, for *au pair* girls from Italy, where the work was on the *Index of Prohibited Books*, not for the sex, but largely because it mocked the clergy.

Giovanni Boccaccio

The Decameron

III, 10

Dear ladies, perhaps you have not heard yet how the devil is put into hell? And therefore, without leaving the subject which you have been discussing all day, I shall tell you how it is done. Perhaps, too, you will find it uplifting and instructive, and may also come to understand that, although love prefers to be in rich palaces and in *chambres separées* rather than in poor men's huts, still it can have its effect and force in wild lands, with tangled forests, alps and lonely caves. And we shall see from this that all things are subject to the power of love.

However, let's come to the point. I must report that there was in the city of Capsa in Arabia a phenomenally rich gentleman who had, among other children, a most beautiful and well-bred young daughter, whose name was Alibech. This girl was not a Christian, but she heard the many Christians who lived in that city commend very highly the Christian faith and the service of God. One day she asked one of them in what way God could be served most easily. He replied that they served God best who fled from the world and from worldly things, like the hermits who lived out in the solitude of the desert.

The young girl, innocent as she was, and about fourteen years of age, set off the following morning to walk to the desert all alone, not after careful thought, but simply on a girlish whim. With some suffering but much firmness on her part she made her way after a few days into the desert and, spotting a little hut in the distance, she made for it and found a holy man at the door, who was extremely surprised to see her there, and asked her what she was looking for. She replied that she had been inspired by God and was looking for a way of serving Him, and someone to teach her how to go about serving God.

The worthy man, who saw how young and beautiful she was, was afraid that if he kept her there the devil might well tempt him, so he praised her good intentions, gave her a small meal of roots, sour apples, dates and water, and then said:

'My daughter, not far from here is a holy man who can teach you what you are looking for much better than I can, so you should go to him.' And he showed her the way to go.

But when she reached that man, she was given the same answer as before, and then, having gone on even further, she came to the cell of a young hermit, a man of piety and devotion, whose name was Rustico, and she asked him the same thing that she had asked the others. Rustico wanted to subject his devotion to a severe testing, so he did not send her away like the others, but kept her with him in his cell. At night he made her a little bed of palm-leaves, and told her to sleep there.

After that, the temptations of the body began to do battle with the forces of steadfastness. Rustico found himself deserted by steadfastness, and came under many attacks before he gave in, and stopped thinking about holy meditation, prayers and discipline, and concentrated instead on the youth and beauty of his companion. He wondered how he could talk to her in such a way that he would not seem to be completely dissolute, but could still get what he wanted. And so, with careful questioning, he established that she had never known a man, and was indeed as innocent as she appeared to be. In view of this he worked out a plan for getting what he fancied under the guise of serving God. First of all he talked to her for a very long time about how the devil is the enemy of God. After that he explained to her that the best way in which she could give service to God was to put the devil in hell, to which God had condemned him.

The girl wanted to know how to do this, to which Rustico replied:

'You will soon know; just do what you see me do.'

With that he took off the few clothes that he was wearing and knelt down, completely naked, and when he did so, the girl took hers off as well, and then knelt down facing him, as if they were going to pray.

Seeing her there, beautiful as she was, Rustico was overcome with desire, and there was a visible resurrection of the flesh, which Alibech noticed, wondered at, and said:

'Rustico, what is that thing which I see you have, but which I haven't got?'

'Oh, my dear daughter,' said Rustico, 'that is the devil I was telling you about. Can you see? He is tormenting me so greatly that I can hardly bear it.'

With that, the girl said:

'God be praised! I can see that I am better off than you are, because I haven't got a devil like that.'

'That's true. But you have something instead that I don't have,' said Rustico.

'What's that?' asked Alibech.

'What you have is hell,' he answered, 'and I tell you that my belief is that God sent you to me for the salvation of my soul, and so that, if this devil goes on tormenting me this way, you will have pity and will let me put him in hell. This will give me great comfort, and will render a great and worthy service to God, if you have indeed come here for that reason, as you told me.'

The girl replied in good faith:

'Oh Father, since I have hell, let us do so whenever you like.'

To this, Rustico replied:

'Bless you, my daughter; so let us go and put him in hell, and maybe he will leave me alone.'

And having said this, he led the girl to one of the narrow beds, and showed her the appropriate position in which they could incarcerate this thing despised by God.

The girl had never put anybody's devil in hell before, and experienced a certain amount of pain the first time, and she said to Father Rustico:

'It's true, Father, this devil really is a wicked fellow and quite properly rejected by God, because there is even pain in hell and its environs when he is put in there.'

'My daughter,' replied Rustico, 'it will not always be like that.'

And to make sure of things, they put him in six times before they moved from the little bed, and by doing it so many times knocked the pride out of his head, so that he would keep the peace.

But it rose again several times after this, and since the girl obediently did her best to control it, it happened that she started to enjoy the game, and she said to Rustico:

'Now I see that what the wise men of Capsa told me was true – that the service of God is sweet. I cannot, indeed, remember doing anything else that gave me so much pleasure and delight as putting the devil into hell. And I reckon that anyone who wants to do anything except this service of God is a fool.'

And because of this she often came to Rustico and said:

'Father, I came here to do service to God, not to be idle. Come on, let us put the devil in hell.'

And while they were doing it, she often said:

'Rustico, I don't know why the devil should ever leave

173

hell. If he were as eager to stay in hell as hell is to receive and hold him, he would never come out again.'

And so the girl kept on inviting and urging Rustico to the service of God, until eventually he was so drained that he felt cold where anyone else would have sweated. And because of this, he told the girl that the devil was not to be castigated or put into hell, unless pride had actually made him rear his head. And – he told her – we, by the grace of God, have so tamed him that he prays God to leave him in peace. And by this he kept the girl quiet.

When the girl saw, however, that he did not want her to come and put the devil in hell, she said to him one day:

'Rustico, your devil has been thoroughly punished and no longer bothers you, but my hell will not let me rest. And so it would be good if you, with the help of your devil, should help ease the anger of my hell, just as I, with my hell, helped you control the pride of your devil.'

Rustico, however, lived on a diet of herbs, roots, and water, and could barely rise to her suggestion. He told her that it would take a lot of devils to do anything about her hell, but that he would do what he could, and he did manage to satisfy her a few times, but so infrequently that it was little more than a drop in the ocean. The girl, meanwhile, not being able to serve God as much as she would have liked, was rather unhappy about it.

At the time when Alibech's hell and Rustico's devil had reached the point of too much desire on the one side, and not enough power on the other, it happened that back in Capsa a fire broke out, and Alibech's father's house was burned down, and he, his sons and the whole family perished with it. Through this, Alibech herself inherited all his wealth. A young nobleman called Neerbale, who had squandered his own entire fortune, found out that she was still alive, looked for her and found her before the government could take over the property on the grounds that the father had died intestate, and took her, much to the delight of Rustico, though against her will, back to Capsa, married her and shared her large inherited fortune. However, before Neerbale had been to bed with her, her ladies asked her how she had served God in the desert, and she told them that she had served him by putting the devil in hell, and that Neerbale had committed a great sin by taking her away from that service.

'How do you put the devil in hell?' asked the ladies.

The girl made it clear to them with words and with gestures, and at this they laughed and laughed again, and then said:

'No need to worry, my dear, that is done here as well. Neerbale will be able to serve God with you very well in that fashion.'

The joke went round the city until it became a popular phrase, that the most pleasing way to serve God is to put the devil in hell. The phrase travelled overseas, even, and it is still current today.

And as for you, dear ladies, if you want God's grace, then make sure you find out how to put the devil in hell, because it pleases God and both of the participants.

And it can bear excellent fruit.

The Monk and the Wee Goose

The fifteenth-century manuscript of German poems now in Karlsruhe that contains the mock Adam and Eve also has this story about a monk. It probably doesn't represent very serious sinfulness; the monk at the centre of it all is too innocent to be wicked, and the abbot (out rent-collecting, probably at Martinmas) is simply unwise. It does show us the Middle Ages not taking monks terribly seriously again, but the real point seems to be the vigorously opportunist attitude of the young lady. She certainly isn't on a pedestal, and knows an opportunity for enjoyment when she sees one. It's rather like the Boccaccio story in reverse.

A Tale from the Karlsruhe Codex

A tale once was told to me
how once there was a monastery
(and it was rich, and well-endowed)
of which the monks could well be proud.
Their house for travellers on their way
did not have fixed times in the day
when food was served. When travellers
on horse or foot came to those doors
they'd find a meal would be waiting
for them, plenty of everything
that they could eat or ask for. Would
that every monastery were as good!
No man was ever turned away.

The gatekeeper had to obey
one rule, and keep that rule in mind,
that no member of *woman*kind
should ever be let through the doors.
The monks spent all their waking hours
on moral thoughts, to live and pray
according to their order's way.

About this place I did hear tell
it was remote, and hidden well,
so that the monks within its rule
but rarely saw a living soul,
and men have told me, furthermore,
that in that monastery were
many who never went outside.

Now one young monk did there reside
who'd spent his whole life in the place,
and who had been there since the days
when he was just a tiny lad.
Because of this, he never had
upon the outside world laid eyes,
and therefore could not recognise
a horse, a cart — all of the ways
that people travelled in those days.

The time of year had come about
when the Abbot had to travel out
on monastery business. So
the young monk begged that he might go
and travel with him, so that he
might see and study the country.
The Abbot gladly granted this —
the young monk's very heartfelt wish;
thanks to his innocence wide-eyed,
the Abbot took him at his side.
The servants now looked after things,
and when the monks were travelling
the horses went at steady pace.

As they got further from that place,
and on the way saw farmyard beasts,
the monk gave the Abbot no rest
but asked him time and time again
to give each animal its name.
The Abbot always answered him,

gave him the name of everything,
like cows or oxen, sheep or lambs,
or even donkeys, pigs and rams.
The Abbot named them, every one.

And when a day's journey was done
they reached a tenant-farmer's land
where an overnight stay was planned.
The yeoman saw them and came out,
and ran and hailed them with a shout:
'Lord Abbot, my welcome to you,
and to all your companions, too!'

When the horses had been cared for,
the monk and Abbot went indoors
to where a fire was burning bright,
for comfort on that wintry night.
There they could take off their shoes
and heavy outer garments, too.

The farmer had a wife, and he
had just one daughter, too, but she
was very beautiful, shapely
and she was aged about twenty.
This daughter, then, had quickly come
to help make the two men at home.
The Abbot bade them all sit down,
now that the day's riding was done.
They all sat down – the daughter too.
The monk said to the Abbot, though
that he should tell him in a word
what *this* new creature might be called?
Quickly the Abbot said: 'Those beasts,
my son? Those creatures are called geese.'
The monk replied: '*Crede mihi,*
those geese look pretty nice to me.
Why is it that we don't keep geese?
They'd fit in well around the place

in our great monastery grounds.'
Then there was laughter all around.
The farmer's daughter and his wife
could not imagine for their life
why this well-built, good-looking youth
could really not know, in all truth,
what *women* were! So straightaway
they asked the Abbot if he'd say
whether the monk was maybe mad?
The Abbot to the ladies said
the things that we've already seen –
how the young monk had always been
inside the monastery. Now when
she heard this tale, the daughter then
took careful note of what was said,
and one thought came into her head:
'This monk is strong and handsome too.
I'd like to see what he can *do*.
Tonight we'll see if this young man
has any idea what you can
do with a girl in bed!' For she
fancied the young monk terribly.

Well now, to keep the story short:
the girl did not reveal her thoughts
nor her intent to anyone.
Late, when the talking was all done,
the monks then wished to take their rest.
The farmer took care of his guests
and ordered beds to be prepared.
The daughter in this business shared,
and she made sure that the young one
was bedded down some distance from
the Abbot, so that he – she said –
could sleep peacefully in his bed.
So everything was done as she
arranged, and wanted it to be.
When the two monks had both retired

the farmer then dismissed his tired
retinue, to take their ease,
and let the monks sleep as they pleased.

The young monk could not sleep at all
because his mind was far too full
of what the names of things had been
which on their journey they had seen.

The girl lay sleepless in her bed
with many thoughts inside *her* head,
like: how was she to carry out
the deeds that she had thought about?
So, once the whole house soundly slept,
she got up, and naked she crept
across to where he lay in bed.
He felt her presence, and he said:
'What's going on? What can this be?'
'It's the young goose,' she said, 'it's me.
I find the night air very chill,
and want to ask you if you will
let me beneath your blankets, please,
to warm myself in case I freeze.
The cold is really so intense.'
The monk, in all his innocence
allowed her, but could not foresee
what the next move in the game would be
when she was settled in there, too.
In fact, the young man could not do
too much at all – he'd no idea
of what they might get up to there
in bedroom play. The girl, though, knew
far better what there was to do,
and thoroughly, and in a short
time, to him all the rules she taught.
The monk then made the fullest use
he could of this willing young goose,
and thought it was the best thing yet!

They played till it began to get
a little close to day, so she
got up and whispered quietly:
'Now, you must never say a word
to anyone of what's occurred
tonight, for if the Abbot knew
he'd very quickly kill the two
of us without thinking.'
She made it very clear to him
that nothing ever must be said.
When he agreed, she left his bed
and went back quickly to her room
full of delight at what she'd done,
and that she'd managed to get there
and nobody had noticed her
slip back into her room once more.
Soon after this it was the hour
of sunrise, and a brand new dawn.
The Abbot didn't lie too long
there in his bed. The monk, smiling,
got up, and they both did the things
that they had come to do, and once
the business was complete and done,
they thought they should no longer stay,
but rather make their homeward way.

When they had reached their home once more
the young monk now came to the fore,
as all the rest came to demand
how he'd enjoyed the outside land.
So he began to tell about
the things they'd seen while they were out,
and thus he told them more and more
of things he'd never seen before.
His talk provided them with fun,
but he was crafty about one
thing, and he never once let slip
about how one night on their trip

181

he'd had a share of goose, and he
had got it absolutely free.
He told no-one (she'd urged him so),
and no-one ever got to know.

But soon that festival fell due
that breaks the winter's dark in two –
yes, Christmas time was close at hand.
The Abbot sent a message, and
summoned the cook and cellarer.
He said: 'Christmas will soon be here,
and we have many tasks to do.
Now,' he went on, 'it's up to you
to see we're well looked after, for
if we are working, then I'm sure
our care needs to be of the best.'
The other monks all acquiesced.

The young monk was not far off, and
he said: 'Sir, if it's your command
that we be well looked after, so
may I suggest something to do?
That you, sir, order if you can
a little goose for every man,
and then I'm sure that no-one would
in all his life feel half as good
again, if he had such a thing.'
The Abbot finished listening,
then called for silence. It was so.
But in a while he said: 'You know,
geese really are the things to take,
the best provision you could make,
the finest thing on earth, I'm sure.'
The Abbot said: 'My son, no more!
Come, brother, no more of this kind
of thing. Have you quite lost your mind,
and gone out of your wits as well?
I'm sure I do not have to tell

you that we eat no meat in here!
Now, show contrition that's sincere,
and do a penance well today.'
The monk he quickly sent away.
And so he left, but still said yet:
'Whatever punishment I get,
if you've a goose, then good for you!
They're really nice, and well-shaped, too.'

They drove him off, quite undismayed.
The cook and cellarer both stayed
and organised what food was due.
And after that they all set to
with prayers and masses, songs and hymns,
and with so many holy things.
But after the last mass was sung,
the Abbot signalled to the young
monk, and he took him to one side,
far from the other monks, in quiet.
He begged the young man earnestly
that he should tell him secretly
very precisely why he had
so clearly said what he *had* said
about the geese, and having one.
The young man saw his earnest tone,
and quickly told him all about
what happened when they had been out,
how, in the night, when on the loose,
he'd got a share of little goose,
and how she'd slipped into his bed
and all the things they'd done and said.
Now when the Abbot heard these words
he sadly sighed, and then answered:
'That was a *girl* – alas for you,
your senseless body lay, it's true,
unlawfully with womankind!
I should have kept all that in mind,
and should have kept an eye on you.'

With that, he told the monk to do
the acts of penance he'd prescribe
for sins committed while outside.

The monk did penance then and there,
but I'm not sure that this was fair!
After all, when the monk was caught
by sin, the Abbot was at fault,
because if he had told the truth
and not made such fun of the youth,
then things would not have gone awry.
It's seldom good to trick or lie,
they're both dishonourable as well.
What more is left for me to tell
that I have not yet said to you?
It's my belief that it is true
that monks exist in this country
—a few, no more than two or three —
who know a bit more than they should
of women — and that's far from good!
Let them do penance, I'd commend;
and here my story's at an end.
The title for the tale I'd choose
is: 'The Monk and the Little Goose,'
because he loved the goose so fair
and all the time was unaware
that he'd been lured into the pit;
but still, he did penance for it
according to the Abbot's word,
and thus atoned where he had erred.

And that's the end! That's all we need
about the crafty goose's deeds!

The Well-Bred English Cock

A very famous poem from a manuscript in the British Library containing songs and carols, mostly in English, written down probably at the start of the fifteenth century. A 1907 anthology drew a comparison with Chaucer's description of Chaunteclere in the *Nun's Priest's Tale*, but this probably isn't the kind of cock intended. It is here adapted a little to get rid of a few archaic and hence now opaque words. *Gentil* means 'noble, well-bred.'

I Have a Gentil Cok

I have a gentle cock
Croweth me day;
He doth me risen early
My matins for to say.

I have a gentle cock
Comes from breeding great;
His comb is of red coral,
His tail is of jet.

I have a gentle cock
Comes of kindred true;
His comb is of red coral
His tail of indigo.

His legs are of azure,
So gentle and so thin,
His spurs are of silver white
Set well into the skin.

His eyes are both of crystal
Locked into amber;
And every night he perches him
In my lady's chamber.

Dafydd ap Gwilym

Something a little less well-bred, and on this occasion Welsh.
There is a whole tradition of priapic poetry, verse that is far
more clearly and specifically dedicated or addressed to the
penis, going back to the Latin *Carmina priapeia*, and moving
on to include folksongs, military and sporting songs, and
blues (though these often hide behind terms like 'jelly-roll'),
as well as Robert Graves' 'Down, Wanton, Down.' Dafydd
ap Gwilym was a fourteenth century Welsh poet, and this
catalogue of boasts is almost certainly by him, though some
editors leave it out, and some manuscripts attribute it to a
contemporary *lady* poet, which misses, so to speak, the point.
The internal rhymes of the Welsh verse-form (*cywydd*) are,
as is the case with all early Welsh verse-forms, completely
impossible to imitate.

Dafydd ap Gwilym

Metrical Verses on the Subject of his Prick

In God's name, prick, I'll have to stand
watch over you with eye and hand,
because you've got me sued, great rod,
I'll always have to be on guard!

On seas of cunt you bob and float,
we'll put a choke-chain on your throat
to rein you, and keep writs at bay,
no matter what the poets say.

You wicked, wicked rolling-pin,
cod-born, don't point up at my chin!
God's gift to ladies everywhere,
the implement they'd store down there,
fine decoy, with a gander's shape,
plumed like a yearling to the nape,

186

wet-headed, with a milky brow,
fast-thrusting shoot – stop growing now!
All bent and blunt, you staff that slides
and slots between a girl's two sides,
you monster-conger, with a hole,
you shaped and turned hazelwood pole,
you're longer than a big man's thigh,
a tool used on a hundred nights,
a bodkin longer than a post,
old leather-prick's the name you boast;
a sceptre, causing lust to come,
bolt-shooting at a girl's bare bum,
an organ pipe runs all the way,
whistle-stop-fucking every day;
you've just one eye, but all the same
you see all women as fair game;
round pizzle-pestle, banging gun
(which sets on fire each little cunt),
a roof-strut for a lady's bower,
a swinging bell that bonks the hour.
Blunt tool, you hoed a fertile row,
skin-trap, long nose with balls in tow,
a trousers-worth of doing wrong,
tough-necked as any goose, and long,
false-hearted spike of wantonness,
you've brought me lawsuits and distress!
A writ for maintenance and keep!
So – down, you baby-planter! Sleep!
I can't keep hold, I can't resist,
you thruster! Wicked thing! Desist!

The wickedness lies in *your* head,
but I, your lord, get blamed instead!

MANNERS

This is another varied heading, and not surprisingly, it includes things on drinking and gambling, just like most of the other sections, and also descriptions of various other excesses, usually in the form of warnings against them, so that potential wickedness can be nipped in the bud.

Sermons are good places to find details of excesses, and the first piece is on gluttony, from a Middle English Franciscan sermon from a manuscript in the Chapter Library at Worcester, dated between 1389 and 1404, the second English one in a mainly Latin collection. The Biblical support is largely omitted in this modernisation.

On excess in eating and drinking, a famous writer, John of Salisbury says in his book *The Policraticon* that the wicked tyrant Dionysius, King of Sicily, was in his youth fair of face, and had a body that was as beautiful and as lovely to look at as any man's that might be found anywhere. But afterwards, when he had indulged in all the lusts and delights of the flesh and especially the love of food and drink, and the misrule that follows on from that, then he lost all his beauty and the strength of his body, and he fell into great sickness and disease, and among other things lost the sight of both eyes. For as John of Salisbury points out, there is nothing in the world that will as soon make a man fall into sickness and to lose his sight as the foul vice of gluttony, that is, excess of food and drink. Therefore for Christ's sake beware of this vice and this sin, especially in the holy season of Lent. And just look at how many men it afflicts with the gout, and to how many folk it gives the dropsy, and brings many other sicknesses upon them before they are aware of it. And then, however much gold they have, and however much silver, because it is incurable they die through the effects of that sickness, and worse – if they die unrepentant, I can state quite firmly that they will be doomed to eternal death at the day of judgement. For even though gold and silver might sometimes help a man or woman in this world to get a doctor to help them from their illness, you can be assured that this will be of no use whatsoever there, because the doctors there have no interest in gold and silver, as the ones on earth do . . . So you can well see that this is a wicked and accursed vice, that not only befouls men and women in this world and brings about bodily death, but also leads afterwards to everlasting death. For there is no leper in the world that seems as foul and horrible in our sight as a glutton in the sight of God. For this doesn't bring men and women into just the one deadly sin, but it makes them fall into many. It makes a man fall first into sloth, for when his belly is so full of food and drink he can do nothing. Sometimes he will be sluggish, sometimes sleepy, at other times too weary to serve God or do any other good work that might profit body and soul. It also makes a man fall into lechery, for when he is overcome with his excesses his reason is eclipsed, and he is ruled only by sensuality that teaches him to desire nothing but lusts and delights of the flesh. Truly, anyone who behaves like that is foully disfigured and robbed of all beauty. [. . .] Also gluttony makes men and women not only blind in the body, but also in the spirit. It leads a man, as you can often see, into drunkenness, and then I tell you he is blind. Though he now sees three candles, yet another man sees but one, and I say he is blind. Truly he may not see what is good and what is evil, and his wits are dulled without and within. He is dulled by his delights in food and drink. I ask you, is this not a great blindness, do you not think, when a man has sat in the ale-house or the tavern all day, yes, and not only all day, but much of the night as well, and at the last he comes home as tight as a tick, shouts at his wife and tells off his children, beats his servants and can barely make it to bed . . .

A Drinking Song

The thirteenth-century manuscript from the Bavarian monastery of Benediktbeuren is probably the most famous collection of songs from the whole Middle Ages, the *Carmina Burana*. This is a short Latin drinking song, with motifs encountered in many other sections of this anthology; it is also about gambling, but as a means of obtaining drinking-money.

Carmina Burana

from Poem 194

> In the boozer
> you're a loser
> if the dice you're shaking.
> You'll get hurt
> and lose your shirt,
> sit there cold and quaking.
> Lady Luck, your gifts are bad,
> you trick us, then you make us mad,
> make us gamble, make us fight,
> and sit out in the cold all night.
>
> 'Brrr!' The naked loser moans,
> when he's cold and left alone,
> shakes and shivers as he groans:
> 'I wish I could be
> asleep under a tree
> With the hot sunshine warming my bones.'
>
> But now let's roll the dice again
> and win some drinking money!
> Who thinks about November's rain
> while it's still warm and sunny?

Bringing up Children

John Lydgate (ca 1370–1449) may or may not have written the *Book of Curteisie*, (also known as *Stans puer ad mensam* – 'The Boy at Table') of which there are various fifteenth-century versions. The large number of books and poems on table and social manners in general give an idea, by telling children *not* to do things, of what people must actually have done on a fairly regular basis. Rampant nose-picking in front of members of the royal family (though 'sovereign' probably just means 'lord') is, of course, hardly in the same category as lust, lechery and drunkenness, but these things have to start *somewhere*. I have modernised, slightly adapted for the sake of modern rhymes, and (because the author really *does* go on a bit) eventually interrupted him in exactly the way he tells his audience not to.

The second poem, *How the Good Wijf taughte Hir Doughtir*, is found in one fifteenth-century manuscript together with the previous work (and also elsewhere). Once again I have modernised, adapted the rhymes (especially for the heavy-handed concluding mottoes), and once more cut it off at about half-time. Not really a text for feminists, although the lines about avoiding public spectacles are good in the original:

> 'Go not to the wrastlinge, ne to shotying at cok
> As it were a strumpet or a giggelot.'

The Book of Polite Behaviour

> My dear son, first yourself enable
> with all your heart to virtuous discipline.
> Before your sovereign, standing at the table
> dispose yourself in line with my doctrine,
> to all nurture your courage to incline.
> First, when you speak, you should not be reckless,
> and keep your hands and fingers still at peace.

Be quite straightforward; do not look aside,
gaze not about, turning around at all,
against a post let not your back abide,
nor make a looking-glass out of the wall.
Pick not your nose; and really above all
be well aware and keep in mind this catch:
before the king, don't rub or pick or scratch.

Whoever speaks to you in any place,
don't cast your head lumpishly down,
but look him clear and solemn in the face.
Walk properly the streets within the town,
and take good heed of wisdom and reason,
that with your wanton laughter you cause no offence
before your lord, when you are in his presence.

Pare clean your nails, and wash your hands also
before you eat, and when you do arise.
Sit in the place that you are assigned to;
Praise not too high in no manner or wise;
And when you see before you the service,
don't be too hasty to bite into bread,
lest 'greedy' is the word that will be said.

Grinning and gawping at table, eschew,
shout not too loud; honestly keep silence.
Stuffing your jaws with food you should not do,
and talking with your mouth full gives offence.
Don't gulp your drink in haste or negligence,
keep clean your lips of flesh and fish;
wipe clean your spoon; don't leave it in the dish.

And with your teeth, of bread do not sops make,
and slurping soup is no gentility:
your cup with dirty mouth you must not take,
and leave no smears, if ale or wine it be;
Don't wipe your filth off on the napery.
Be sure that when at meals you start no strife,

194

don't pick your teeth at table with your knife.

Just honest mirth should be your dalliance;
but do not swear, and speak no ribaldry.
The best morsels – keep this in remembrance –
don't garner for yourself exclusively.
Share with your fellows, that's gentility.
Let not your plate be piled high with food,
make sure your nails aren't black, but clean and good.

It is against the rules for gentlemen,
by telling lies, to cause offence;
don't bring old scores to light again;
approach your lord with reverence.
Don't play with your knife, learn some sense;
Keep still and quiet when you eat,
and never shuffle with your feet.

Don't spill your sauce or splash the soup,
don't bring a dirty knife to table,
don't fill your spoon, lest it should drop
beside you (*not* commendable!)
Be quick and sharp, willing and able,
ready to fulfil right away
anything that your lord should say.

And anywhere you dine or sup
take salt politely with your knife,
make sure you don't blow in your cup,
be friendly and begin no strife.
Try to stay peaceful all your life.
Don't interrupt a man, where'er you wend,
before he brings his tale to an end . . .

The good wife taught her daughter
full many a time and oft,
a good woman to be,
and said: 'My daughter dear,
some good things you must hear,
if you listen to me.

Daughter, if you want to be a wife,
make sure you wisely work,
look lovely and lead a good life,
love God and Holy Church.
Go to church whenever you may
—make sure that you have been —
for you will do better on a day
when God's house you have seen.
He must surely ever thrive
who lives decently all his life
my dear child.

Gladly pay tithes and taxes both,
to care for the poor be not loth,
give generously, be not hard,
a house will prosper where God is steward.
They merit more
who love the poor
my dear child.

When you sit in Church, just tell your beads,
don't chatter with your friends instead,
don't laugh at others, old or young,
bear yourself well and keep your tongue;
behave like this,
your worship will increase,
my dear child.

If any man courts you and wants to marry,

take care not to scorn him, whatever he be,
but talk to your friends, don't hide it from them.
But don't get so close that you're tempted to sin.
For a slander raised ill,
is very hard to quell,
my dear child.

The man you shall wed before God with a ring,
love him and honour above all earthly things;
meekly you must answer, not assertively,
then you'll calm his mood, and his darling you'll be.
A fair word and meek
lays wrath to sleep
my dear child.

Fair of speech you should be, glad, and of mild mood,
true in words and in deed, and in your conscience good;
keep away from sin, villainy and blame,
and do not let others speak of you with shame;
if a good life you lead
you'll not be in need,
my dear child.

Be seemly and wise, keep your manners in mind,
and don't change your looks just as you change your mind;
do not be a slut, though, whatever betide,
don't laugh too loudly and don't yawn too wide,
but laugh soft and mild
and don't be too wild
my dear child.

Outside, don't walk too rapidly,
nor toss your head, or wiggle your body;
don't talk too much, and do not swear –
such manners lead to wickedness, I fear;
for to get a bad name
is the wrong kind of fame,
my dear child.

Don't go into town just on some pretext,
gadding about from one house to the next,
don't go to the market to sell your fine cloth,
then straight to the tavern to spend the whole lot.
To the tavern to drift,
isn't good for your thrift
my dear child.

If you're in the vicinity of some good beer,
whether you are serving or supping the cheer,
drink moderately, and you won't get the blame
of being a drunk, which leads only to shame.
If you're often in drink
then your money will sink,
my dear child.

Don't go to the wrestling, or shooting or darts,
these are fit only for strumpets and tarts.
Stay at home, daughter, and love thy work, too,
and then, my dear child, riches will come to you.
Far better is the one intent
with what one has, to be content
my dear child.

Don't stop to chat with each young man that you meet,
say 'good day' and move on, when you pass in the street.
Then let him move on – do not stand there and chat,
so he gets no ideas to do lots more than that!
For a man may tell lies
that fair words can disguise,
my dear child . . .'

Sebastian Brant

Brant's *Narrenschiff*, the *Ship of Fools*, appeared in 1494 and is one of the most famous works of its time – much reprinted and much translated. Brant attacks over a hundred types of foolishness, and this section shows the regularity of it all, as he hits out at a couple of fashion standbys: effeminate men (with medallions), and miniskirts. (The reference in this translation to a 'Christmas Tree' *is* an anachronism, but the original reference would have needed a footnote.)

Sebastian Brant

The Ship of Fools

IV. THE LATEST FASHIONS

If you are one of fashion's slaves,
your action ruins and depraves,
and you're one of the fools and knaves.

What used to be despised before
no-one cares about any more.
Men wore their beards with pride a while,
but now they're learning women's styles,
and smear cold cream upon their face,
and on their bare necks (ringed with lace)
medallions on chains we see
(as if they were a Christmas Tree).
They put pomade upon their hair
and then back-comb it everywhere.
They sit there with the curling-tongs,
or spread their hair out in the sun,
or bleach it by the fire all day,
(and let the lice come out and play).
They seem to dress in comfort, though,
with pleated clothes and furbelows,

doublets and jackets, shirts, cravats,
silk slippers, boots, hose, shoes and hats,
fur collars, long coats, all the same,
everything foreign's 'in' again.
One fashion comes, another goes,
what fools we are is all it shows,
and capable of anything,
each novelty that fashion brings,
with skirts so shamefully cut short,
they barely cover what they ought.
It piles shame on me and you,
exposing bits not meant for view,
and showing what good taste conceals.
So things are really bad, I feel,
and I'm quite sure that they'll get worse,
so, fashion-followers, be cursed!
And if you, too, ignore this wrong,
then *you'll* get caught, before too long.

Andrew Boorde

Boorde was born right at the end of the Middle Ages, at the start of the sixteenth century, and we don't know a great deal about him; he studied medicine, spent a certain amount of time in the Tower and one or two other prisons, got drunk in Monpellier in 1542, wrote a controversial treatise against beards, and was once accused of keeping three whores at Winchester. But he did write a fascinating tourist handbook of Britain, the *First Boke of the Introduction of Knowledge*, dedicated to Princess (later either 'Queen' or 'Bloody') Mary, published in 1547. I have selected the section on Cornwall (here adapted and modernised), not because of the adverse and probably quite unjust comments on sixteenth-century Cornish food or beer, and certainly not for the 'enjoy yourself' philosophy, but because Boorde puts his finger on one of the *real* signs of decadence in any society: an unholy urge to take each other (Cornishmen, that is, whose names begin with Tre-, Pol-or Pen-) to court all the time, usually about trivial nonsense.

Andrew Boorde

The First Book of the Introduction of Knowledge

The appendix to the first chapter, treating of Cornwall and Cornishmen

> I am a Cornishman, ale I can brew;
>> It will make one to cack, also to spew.
> It is thick and smoky, and sometimes it is thin,
>> It is like wash that hogs have wrestled in.
> I cannot brew, nor prepare meat or fish,
>> Many folk say I mar many a dish.
> Close the door, mate, I've something to say:
>> 'When old knaves are dead, young knaves will play.'
> I'm starving to death, I swear by my faith,

I've eaten no meat since yesterday;
I should really like to take a cup –
    Give me a quart of ale to sup!
Good mate, at home I've fish and tin,
    Drink, mate, with me, or else I'll begin.
God, what great cold and hunger I abide!
    Will you, friend, come home at the next tide?
I pray God to preserve him well,
    That when he comes home, me he will not kill
For putting a straw through his great net.
    Another pot of ale, mate, now for me fetch.
I'll go off to London to try at the law,
    And sue Tre-, Pol- and Pen- for wagging a straw.
Now fellow, farewell, I can no more abide,
    I'm off to the alehouse on the other side.
So come now with me, fellow I pray,
    And let us make merry as long as we may.

Cornwall is a poor and very barren country of all manner of
things except tin and fish. Their meat, their bread and drink
is marred and spoilt for lack of good ordering and dressing.
Fir-cones and turves are their chief fuel. Their beer is absolutely worthless, looking white and thick, as if pigs had
wrestled in it.

    Smoky and ropey
    never a good sup
    in most places it's worse and worse,
    pity it is, them to curse.
    For wagging of a straw
    they will go to law,
    and all not worth a haw,
    playing like a jackdaw.

202

RELIGION

The Middle Ages are often seen as 'the age of belief,' and the period did of course produce literary works of genuine and – in the best sense of the term – monumental Christian piety: Dante is well enough known, Wolfram von Eschenbach's *Parzival* and Hartmann von Aue's *Gregorius* (undeservedly) less so. But there was another side. Church pronouncements against various kinds of spells indicate the ongoing use of magic, even if we have to exclude the many healing charms, which usually came equipped with a couple of 'Our Fathers' as insurance and were therefore, broadly speaking, acceptable. Storm raising and cursing are often mentioned, and people *do* seem to have tried to invoke demons, although it certainly did Gilles de Rais no good. On the other hand, a bargain with the devil *could* enhance one's career prospects. There are plenty of legends of pacts with the devil, culminating of course in the Faust story. The devil nearly always wins, except in those versions where the pact-maker invokes the Virgin (or, in Goethe's case, perhaps, the Eternal-Feminine). This is the saving of Theophilus, whose story is very close to the later one of Pope Joan (the Papacy was apparently filled, with diabolical assistance, by a woman, who gave the game away somewhat by giving birth in the Vatican, but who still went to heaven). But much of the material is presented as a warning, and black masses were probably not *really* held in Cornwall. Parody is another matter, though, and mock liturgies abound – the literary equivalents of the gargoyle. And at the end of the Middle Ages came the Reformation, based on the views held by the new Protestants that the Catholic Church had become decadent; not surprisingly, however, the Catholic Church took a similar view of the ideas put forward by the new Protestants, and consigned Luther to the privy.

The first example, however, *is* concerned with Black Magic. There is evidence, largely provided by the complaints of the official Church, of the use of black magic for various pragmatic purposes. These examples come from a tenth-century Latin Penitential (probably by Burchard of Worms), a series of questions addressed to the would-be penitent, and the questions give an idea of what must have been in people's minds. Some are (very much) odder than others.

65, 68, 103, 151, 172, 180, 186

Hast thou behaved as certain adulterous women are said to do? As soon as they see that their lovers wish to take lawful wedded wives, they ensure by certain black magical arts that the male vigours of the men are extinguished, so that they cannot please their lawful wives, nor make love to them. (If you have done this, or taught others to do so, the penance is forty days on bread and water.)

Hast thou done as certain women are said to do? They take a live fish and place it in their privy parts until it is dead, then serve it boiled or roasted to their husbands. They do this in order to increase the husband's ardour for them.

Hast thou believed, or ever fallen into the perfidy of thinking that those conjurors who claim to be able to raise storms may indeed be able to conjure up storms or demons by incantation, or that they may be able to affect the minds of men?

Hast thou ever collected herbs for medicinal purposes, and whilst doing chanted wicked magic spells, and not liturgical or holy ones, such as the Creed or the Our Father?

Hast thou ever done what certain women are said to have done? If they have a child which dies unbaptised, they take the corpse and put it in a secret place, and place a stake through the tiny body, saying that if they do not, then the little child will rise up and cause much damage.

Hast thou ever made little toys, or toy bows, or small tools, and placed them in the cellar or in the storeroom, so that goblins and demons can play with them there, and will then be favourable to you in other things?

Hast thou ever believed, as certain people are said to believe, that those women commonly known as the Fates exist, or are able to do what is believed of them, namely that when a man is born, that they can change him into anything he wants, and that there are some men who can at will change themselves into wolves – they are known as 'werewolves' in the Germanic tongue – or into other things?

Rutebeuf

The French professional poet known only as Rutebeuf was probably born in Paris and certainly worked there in the second half of the thirteenth century, producing an extensive amount of material. His work includes several poems, and a version of one of them was recorded by Joan Baez in the 'sixties under the title of 'Pauvre Rutebeuf.' This dramatisation is of one of the better-known legends of the Middle Ages, which originated in Greek, went into Latin by the ninth century and turns up in most European languages, including Low German. Theophilus of Cilicia is a medieval Faustus (just like Marlowe's), who gets ahead (or rather, is restored to his former position) by rejecting God for the devil. But after seven years he does have the sense to repent – this is rather earlier, in fact than many, and some never make it at all. The Virgin Mary turns this into a miracle, even though the devil prudently got it all in writing.

Rutebeuf

The Miracle Play of Theophilus

begins here:

THEOPHILUS
>Alas, my God and glory-king,
>I've always spent my time thinking
>of you. I've given more and more,
>yes, all my good, to help the poor,
>and what's left isn't worth a flea!
>The Bishop has said 'check' to me,
>then cornered me and said 'checkmate,'
>and left me in a sorry state.
>Now I shall have to starve instead,
>or sell my robe to buy some bread.
>Then where will all my household go?

Will God protect them? I don't know!
God? Well, what's *He* going to do?
They'll have to go off somewhere new.
God's ears are deaf to me today –
He doesn't hear a word I say.
Well, I'll just cock a snook at Him
and curse all of His following!
There's nothing that I wouldn't do
to earn (stuff God!) a bob or two.
What, should I hang myself, or drown?
After all, I can't pull God down
and shout at Him. He's out of reach.
Dammit, if you could just impeach
Him, or give him a hefty clout,
that would be worth bragging about.
But He has hidden in the skies
away from all his enemies,
so they can't grab or injure him.
If I could just be threatening
towards God, skirmish with him, or fight,
I'd leave him shivering with fright!
He's living well up there, you know,
while I'm abandoned here below
in poverty and suffering.
My fiddle hasn't got a string!
They'll say that I've gone quite crazy
and then they'll mock and laugh at me,
and soon I'll find that I won't dare
to mix with people anywhere
because they'll point the finger, too.
I've no idea what I should do.
Yes, God's treated me like a cad!

[Theophilus goes to visit Salatin, who is able to speak with demons whenever he pleases]

SALATIN

What's this, Theophilus, so sad?
In God's name, what disastrous fall

208

has made you look so miserable –
you used to be so well before!

THEOPHILUS

They used to call me 'Master' or
'My Lord' here (as I'm sure you know),
but now they've really laid me low.
And, Salatin, what's so unfair
is that I've always said a prayer
in French or Latin every day
to Him, who's taken it away!
He's left me stripped and quite bereft
of everything – I've nothing left.
So now there's nothing I'd not do
(however strange, however new –
I'd take it on without a word!)
if my position were restored.
Its loss means pain and shame to me.

SALATIN

My friend, your troubles I can see.
A man who once had wealth to show
will suffer much distress and woe
when he's reduced to charity
to beg his food and drink, and he
must listen as they call him names.

THEOPHILUS

That's just what causes me such pain,
Salatin, dearest, dearest friend –
that I on others must depend!
It nearly breaks my heart in two.

SALATIN

I know it must be hard for you
to be in such a sorry state,
a man as noble and as great
as you – it must be hard indeed.

THEOPHILUS

Salatin, be a friend in need
and tell me if you know how I
can possibly recover my

position, honour, status too.
There's nothing that I wouldn't do.

SALATIN

Would you renounce the God that you
so long and often have prayed to?
And all His saints and sanctity,
and, with clasped hands, could you then be
the servant of a different lord,
by whom all things would be restored?
And yet more honours would accrue
if you became *his* servant true.

THEOPHILUS

I'd do all that and gladly, too!
Just ask and I'll do all you please.

SALATIN

Off you go, then, and be at ease.
Whatever power they possess,
I'll get your post back, nonetheless.
Come back tomorrow and see me.

THEOPHILUS

Salatin, I shall, willingly.
May that god in whom you believe
guard you, if this goal we achieve.

[Theophilus leaves Salatin, but it occurs to him that renouncing God is a very serious step]

THEOPHILUS

Alas, what will become of me
I've sunk into insanity
if this is how it has to be!
    What shall I do
if Saint Nicholas I eschew,
and Saint John and Saint Thomas too,
    and sweet Mary?
Now what of the soul within me?
In flames it will burn certainly
    in hell so black.
And I nevermore shall come back,

but be kept there forever! Oh, alack!
    It's not some tale!
In that fire, which is eternal,
there are no proper folk at all,
just evil ones and the devil.
    It's their nature –
they live in darkness so obscure
no sunbeams penetrate their door,
and everything's filth and manure.
    Damned already!
If now I change so thoroughly,
go on with my apostasy,
then God will turn His back on me.
    Barred from his sight!
And He'd have cause enough, and right.
No man was ever in such plight
    as I am here!
Still – Salatin's offer is dear,
giving me back my goods and power,
with no-one any the wiser . . .
    So, let it be!
I'll hurt God as He has hurt me;
I'll no more serve him! Let Him be!
    I'll hurt him more!
I shall be rich where now I'm poor.
He hates me? I'll hate Him for sure.
    It's in His hand.
Wars can begin at His command,
He holds the sea and sky and land,
    But I'll break free
if what Salatin promised me
    is realised.

[Here, Salatin speaks to the devil, and says:]

SALATIN
        A Christian came to me, and sighed.
        I've tried to keep him satisfied,
        but now you must be at my side.

211

Satan, you hear?
He'll come tomorrow, never fear,
I've promised him and had to swear
   that you'll await.
He used to be of great estate,
and is a prize that we should rate,
so do his bidding as the bait.
   Do you agree?
I'll have to make you come to me:
   I conjure thee!
and at nightfall, come rapidly,
delay will hurt us both, you see,
   to me, I say!

[Salatin invokes the devil]

Bagahi laka bachahay
lamech cahi achabahay
   kyrie-aloss.
Lamech, lamech bachalioss,
cabahagi sabbalioss
   Bari-olas.
Lagozatha cabyolas
Samahac et famyolas
   Harrahyee!

[The devil which he has conjured by this spell now appears]

DEVIL

You spoke that spell effectively,
remembered all the words, I see,
   to what avail?

SALATIN

No, now you cannot let me fail,
nor try to go against my will
   when I call you.
I'm going to make you sweat for use.
You want to know the latest news?
   A cleric's ours!
We've had our eye on him for years,

212

he's often caused us grief and tears
　　with all his deeds.
Whom do you think this cleric needs,
and for our help now strongly pleads?

DEVIL

　　What is his name?

SALATIN

Theophilus is this man's name,
and very widespread is his fame
　　in all the land.

DEVIL

With him I've often tried my hand,
but he was not mine to command.
But since to come to *us* he's planned,
　　let's have him in,
without a horse, without his kin –
that will be no hardship for him –
　　it's very near.
He'll be made welcome, never fear,
by Satan and the devils here.
　　Don't let him pray
to Jesus, Mary's son. I say
he'll get no help there anyway.
　　And now I'll flee.
You must treat me with courtesy
and for a month not bother me.
　　Go, Salatin –
no Hebrew now, and no Latin!

[Theophilus comes back to see Salatin as arranged]

THEOPHILUS

Is this too soon in the morning?
　　No news for me?

SALATIN

I've seen to your case rapidly,
and those who harmed you so badly
　　will now restore
your rank, and honours on you pour

213

to make you greater than before
    you ever were.
You won't be poor and wretched here,
but noble once again, I swear.
    Don't be afraid.
You must go down – don't be delayed
(it won't help if to God you prayed
    don't ask Him now!)
If you need some support somehow
He never helped you anyhow
    but failed you.
He treated you most cruelly, too,
and caused you pain ever anew,
    till I stepped in!
The devils wait – come on within
    this very hour.
Don't think of God, He's got no power.

THEOPHILUS

I'll go. God cannot hurt me now
    nor aid, indeed.
So I'll no longer pray and plead.

[Theophilus goes down to the devil in great trepidation, and the devil says to him:]

DEVIL

Come on now, quick, keep on the move,
don't make me think you need a shove,
like some poor peasant off to pay a bill.
What is demanded by your master, tell –
I know he is a proud man, that's for sure.

THEOPHILUS

Indeed, my lord, he is the chancellor,
and he would like to put me on the streets
to beg, and so you I beseech
to help me in my very hour of need.

DEVIL

You ask me truly?

214

THEOPHILUS

> Yes.

DEVIL

> Indeed,
> you must do homage then to me,
> and I shall help generously.

THEOPHILUS

> In feudal homage I give you my hand.
> Just let me get my goods again,
> then fealty I shall owe to you.

DEVIL

> Well, here's the covenant between us two.
> I shall make you a lord so great
> that no-one's been of such estate.
> Then, since it's your avowed intent,
> you know I'll need a covenant,
> with letters drawn and signed by you,
> and fully sealed and witnessed, too.
> I've been deceived by folk before,
> forgetting to bind them by law.
> That's why it has to be done right.

THEOPHILUS

> Here – you will find it's watertight!

[Theophilus gives the letter to the devil – *we hear later that it is signed in blood* – and the devil tells him how to behave]

DEVIL

> My very dear Theophilus,
> now you've sworn fealty to us,
> I'll tell you how you have to be:
> on beggars do not waste pity,
> if some poor wretch asks you to pay,
> cock a deaf ear and walk away;
> if you're treated with courtesy,
> respond with pride, imperiously;
> if some poor man comes to your lands,
> let him get nothing from your hands.
> Kindness, humility, pity,

and friendship and sweet charity
and fasting, penance – all that lot
just give me a burning gut-rot.
Alms-giving and saying your prayers,
reduce me both to angry tears,
whilst loving God and chastity
are like a serpent gnawing me,
eating my heart and belly through!
And visiting hospitals, too,
to visit somebody who's ill,
that makes *me* faint and tremble still,
makes my heart beat erratically,
yes, doing good just torments me.
Go back. They'll make you seneschal,
but don't do good – just do evil.
Mind your judgements are never fair,
for that won't get you anywhere,
and to me you would be untrue.

THEOPHILUS

I'll do just what I have to do.
It's only right to do your will
if I'm to be restored in full.

[At this point the bishop sends someone to look for
Theophilus]

BISHOP

Pincher, can you leave instantly
and find Theophilus for me?
His powers I must now restore;
I acted foolishly, I'm sure
when I tried to take them away.
He is such a fine man, I say,
I don't know what came over me!

PINCHER

My lord, it's true, I do agree.

[Pincher the servant speaks to Theophilus, who replies:]

216

PINCHER

    Who's there?

THEOPHILUS

    Say who *you* are, at least.

PINCHER

    The bishop's clerk.

THEOPHILUS

    And I'm a priest.

PINCHER

    Theophilus, my lord, I ask
    that you should not take me to task.
    The bishop is asking for you
    and wants to give you back your due,
    your living and your whole stipend,
    and so you should rejoice, my friend,
    that's the right thing for you to do.

THEOPHILUS

    The devil take both him and you!
    I should have been the bishop, me!
    But I invested him. Folly!
    We quarrelled when he took the throne,
    and then he tried me to disown.
    Well damn him then, for all his hate,
    and his whingeing that won't abate!
    But still I'll go, give it a trial.

PINCHER

    When he sees you, he's bound to smile
    and say that it was just a test
    of faith. Then he'll restore the rest,
    and be your friend, just as before.

THEOPHILUS

    But he's got mass-priests by the score
    whose lies have all blackened my name.
    The devil take them, all the same!

[The bishop rises when Theophilus comes in, and restores him to his office, saying:]

BISHOP

Sir, I am glad to see you here.

THEOPHILUS

I can fend for myself, I'm sure,
I haven't dropped off, anyhow!

BISHOP

Dear sir, I want to give back now
what I deprived you of, and make
amends, and beg you now to take
your office back. Take it from me,
you are a worthy man, I see,
so what I have belongs to you.

THEOPHILUS

You know your paternoster too,
better than those you've said before.
Now, I suppose, score upon score
of peasantry and hoi polloi,
will come in hundreds to enjoy
my favour? Well, I'll make them kneel!
It's fear, not honour that appeals.
I'll treat them with a fine disdain.

BISHOP

Theophilus, what can you mean?
Dear friend, think just of good to do!
Come, look inside your lodging new,
your residence is next to me –
our wealth and all our property
we shall hold jointly evermore;
we must be friends, of that I'm sure.
What's mine is yours, what's yours is mine.

THEOPHILUS

Indeed, sir, that seems very fine.

[Now Theophilus goes out and quarrels with his
companions – starting with one named Peter]

THEOPHILUS

Peter, d'you want to hear what's new?
How fortune's wheel has turned for you?

218

The hand you've drawn is really bad –
hold on to what you've got, my lad –
you won't get my job after all,
the bishop thought he would recall
me – so no thanks to you, I fear!

PETER

Theophilus, what's this I hear?
Not threats? Why only yesterday
I asked him to recall you straightaway,
because that seemed both right and fair.

THEOPHILUS

Oh yes, you made a slip-up there,
in getting me ejected then.
In spite of you, I'm back again.
You never gave a thought to me!

PETER

But sir, I swear vigorously
I wanted you for bishop when
the former bishop died, but then
you said you didn't want the job,
you were too much in awe of God.

[Theophilus shifts his attention to someone else]

THEOPHILUS

Thomas, Thomas, you'll feel the pain
now I'm your seneschal again.
You'll have to pull your socks up now,
give up your nonsense anyhow.
I'll be the worst taskmaster yet.

THOMAS

Theophilus, I could just bet
you look as if you've drunk a bit.

THEOPHILUS

What, insults too? Oh well, that's it
You're out tomorrow! Good riddance!

THOMAS

In God's name! Are you in a trance?
I love you and respect you too!

219

THEOPHILUS
  Thomas, I'll spell it out to you:
  it's up to me who stays or goes.
THOMAS
  You've become very bellicose!
  Leave me and speak to me no more.
THEOPHILUS
  Thomas, you try my patience sore!
  You'll sweat and plead, my little man,
  before I've finished, that's my plan.

[But Theophilus now repents, and goes into a Lady Chapel
and says:]

  Alas, odious wretch, what will become of me?
  Earth, can you bear to feel the weight I put on thee?
  I gave up my true God for vain apostasy,
  and took as lord a prince of purest misery.

  God I renounced – I can't conceal it any more,
  I threw away the balm, the fruit I chose was sour,
  I signed away the deed and perished in that hour
  and now my soul will have to pay the debt for sure.

  O God, what will you do with this unhappy knave,
  whose soul is bound for fiery hell, the devil's slave,
  where devil's feet take vengeance for my sin so grave?
  Earth, swallow me! Hide me! Nothing more can me save.

  Lord God, what can such a foul, wicked creature do,
  despised by God and all the world, and by men too,
  betrayed and trapped in fiery hell by demons who
  will torture him with fire for ever and anew.

  Alas, I once was full of pride and ignorance
  when I rejected God for one small lucky chance,
  the riches of the world which so did me entrance,
  have cast me into hell, damned me without a glance.

Satan, full seven years I've complied eagerly,
the wicked songs you made me sing so merrily
I've sung; but I committed many a felony;
in hell my flesh must pay for all that misery.

Souls must be loved, but for mine no-one had a share.
I dare not ask Our Blessed Lady for her care.
Some seeds don't grow, when they are sown amongst the
   tares,
and thus my soul – and hell awaits my last despair.

Alas, how stupidly I've served and I've been served,
and what pains now for me and my soul are reserved.
To ask Our Lady's help is more than I've deserved,
yet she might serve to save my soul if her I'd served!

In dirt I'm dyed, and in the filth and in ordure
I'll die as I have lived – in dirt then, I'll endure
enduring hell; God lives. But I shall die for sure;
devils will surely beat me direly at death's door.

In heaven or on earth there's nowhere I can hide.
Alas, what place on earth would now take me inside?
Of being damned always in hell I'm terrified;
no paradise for me, though, since God I denied.

I dare not call on God nor on His saints depend,
since I have offered all my service to the fiend.
The devil has the pact and covenant I signed;
I got my riches, but I must have been quite blind.

I dare not call on God, the saints I cannot name,
nor on Our Lady full of grace, to whom all fame
is due. But since in her there is no hint of blame
I'll turn to her for help in spite of all my shame.

[And now follows the prayer which Theophilus directed to
the Virgin Mary:]

Queen of the skies
Virgin most wise
Lady full of grace
from whom virtues arise,
to you my heart flies;
deliver us apace,
we gaze on your face
with sweetest surprise;
fountain, fair place,
of noblest race
may your Son hear my sighs.

From sweet service of you
they seduced me, it's true,
tempted thoroughly,
by the foul devil who
(evil through and through)
cast a spell over me.
Lady, set me free,
for your charity
is pure, and can do
wonders, or my body
will be in misery
when hell claims its due.

Sweet Lady Mary
my heart change for me
so that I serve you,
or I'll never be free
from all my misery.
Take my soul, too,
which deserves death, it's true.
When the devil comes to
take me, have pity,
and help my soul through.
Body's pain is fair due
for the soul's liberty.

Lady of charity,
Maid of humility,
our salvation you bore
which from death set us free,
from pain and cruelty,
now and for evermore.
Praises on you I pour
Lady, blessings and more,
now I know verily!
Lady, let me be sure
I'm not damned evermore
to hell's eternity.

Hell's gates are open wide
to welcome me inside
for my soul's wicked sin;
I should be terrified
if I now should be tied
and if I were shut in.
Lady, homage I bring
look upon me within,
in spite of all my pride
for your Son, yes for Him,
don't let devils deride
or hell be satisfied!

You are like a pane
of glass; light comes again
all unbroken through.
You a virgin remained
though into you God came,
a bride and mother too.
O most shining jewel,
Lady, tender and true,
hear my prayer and my pain,
keep my body and soul
from the fires so cruel,
let me love you again.

O Queen full of grace,
bring light to this place
and the dark drive away!
Into favour me raise
let me work all my days
to please you every way.
I've been too long astray
on the paths of dismay.
Still the demons of hate
want to take me today.
Lady, to you I pray
keep me from this disgrace.

My life was impure.
In filth and ordure
for too long I have been.
Lady, spotless and pure
do grant me your cure,
and heal me again;
with your treatment divine
make my heart free of pain
with the love that endures.
Most beautiful queen
dazzle me with your gleam
lead me into your care.

The fiends wickedly
caught me up, and I'll be
torn asunder one day.
They are torturing me
Lady, I can be free
if your Son will but say!
Lady to you I pray –
you know I've gone astray –
don't give them victory.
All the world's in your sway
hide my poor soul away
where no devil can see!

OUR LADY

> Who are you? And what brings you here?

THEOPHILUS

> Have pity on me, Lady dear!
>> I am the wretch
> Theophilus, whom men reject,
> and whom the devils want to fetch.
>> I come to pray
> to you, My Lady, and to say
> that I can never get away
>> from agony
> with Satan who so torments me.
> Once, long ago, you smiled on me,
>> O queen most dear.

OUR LADY

> Your babbling I don't want to hear!
> Out of my chapel! Out of here!

THEOPHILUS

>> I do not dare!
> Rose, eglantine and lily fair,
> you who the Son of God did bear,
>> what can I do?
> I've bound myself up like a fool
> with the devil, who's angry, too!
>> I've no idea,
> so I cannot cease in my prayer,
> sweet Lady, blithe and debonaire,
>> most honoured Maid,
> lest my soul is to be displayed
> in hell, and there forever stay,
>> with Satan's crew!

OUR LADY

> Theophilus, I once knew you!
> You used to be my servant, too,
>> so now, believe!
> Your covenant I shall retrieve
> which you made when you were naive,
>> I'll find a way.

[Our Lady now goes to retrieve the covenant made by
Theophilus]

OUR LADY

  Satan, Satan, come out, I say!
  If you've come to the world today,
  to battle for my cleric – nay,
   this cannot be!
  Give his covenant back to me,
  you've gone too far in villainy.

SATAN

   Out of my hands?
  I'm hanged if you'll get that covenant!
  I got his job back for him, and
  he swore that he'd take my command
   quite willingly,
  granting body and soul to me.

OUR LADY

  Then I shall smite you mightily!

[And now Our Lady takes the covenant back to Theophilus,
saying:]

  My friend, your covenant I bring,
  although it was a close-run thing
  and you nearly beyond saving.
   Hear what I say:
  go to the bishop, no delay,
  give him the covenant today
   to read aloud
  in church, before a mighty crowd,
  so other good men are not cowed
   by such deceit.
  A man whose love of wealth, whose greed,
  betrays him is shameful indeed.

THEOPHILUS

  Lady, I will!
  Body and soul are swiftly killed
  by fruits of seeds sown in evil,

I see that now!

[Theophilus now goes to the bishop and gives him the covenant, saying:]

Sir, hear me now, I pray, listen,
I come to you despite my sin!
   and you shall know
just what it was oppressed me so.
I was cast naked in the snow
   by poverty.
The devil lies in wait, and he
took my soul off most wickedly.
   I ought to fall.
But Our Lady, who loves us all
turned me from the path infernal,
   from the road where
I was wandering in despair
towards the devil, waiting there
   in darkest hell,
the one who'd made me turn as well
from God, and all good works repel
   just for his sake!
The covenant I had to make
was sealed so that it could not break.
   It hurt, alack,
I thought my very heart would crack;
but then Our Lady brought it back,
   God's mother dear,
whose virtue shines out bright and clear.
Father, I beg you, don't forbear
   the text to read.
so other men are not destroyed
and from the true path led aside
   by such treason.

[The bishop reads the covenant and then says aloud:]

BISHOP

Hear me, for Christ the Virgin's Son,

of what Theophilus, good sirs, has done,
   and hear me well!
For he was tricked by the devil,
— this is all true as the Gospel,
   so mark it, too!
It's only right I should tell you
so listen, and that's what I'll do.

'All those who hear this covenant should learn
how I, Satan, caused Fortune's wheel to turn;
Theophilus by his bishop was spurned,
who took his wealth and none of it returned.

At this outrage, Theophilus went angrily
to Salatin, and raged despairingly,
and said that he would do homage to me
if I'd restore his wealth and dignity.

He'd led a holy life thus far; again
and then again I'd tempted, but in vain,
till he came begging to me in his pain.
He did homage, and got his wealth again.

The covenant was sealed with his own ring,
and his own blood was used for the writing,
not ink, and then I promised everything.
Then his dignity was restored to him.'

This good Christian was trapped indeed,
but now again he has been freed
   by God's handmaid.
Mary the Virgin, undismayed
brought him out of the trap he'd made,
so let us all now, in our praise
   for this great thing
stand and *Te deum laudamus* sing!

THUS ENDS THE MIRACLE OF THEOPHILUS.

A Black Mass

Not surprisingly, we don't have too many records of *actual* black masses. This mock one, from a play in Cornish, is designed to frighten anyone inclined to put his or her trust in the forces of darkness. These were often viewed in the Middle Ages as a grotesque conglomerate of satanism, a misunderstood and (since it is actually not polytheistic) ignorantly maligned Islam, and classical mythology. Written in around 1500, the *Life of St Meriasek* is a two-day play cycle showing us the deeds of the Breton St Mereadoc (and his adventures in Cornwall). In an integrated but separate story, a young Christian is captured by a pagan tyrant king, whose hard-drinking but underpaid and bullied torturers go in for devil-worship. Incidentally, the lad is rescued miraculously by the Virgin after a little celestial blackmail by his mother, who removes the statue of the Christ-child from a church and holds it as a hostage. The torturers go (presumably) to hell.

The Cornish Life of St Meriasek

FIRST DEMON

  Peace, I say, to wild and tame,
  I say Moufras is my name;
  never had I any shame
  furthering sin.
  Lots of servants work for me,
  worshipping me busily.
  One day I'll lock'em all in!

SECOND DEMON

  With your tricks and with your spells
  you catch people very well,
  but I'm worse yet!
  My name is Shirlywit
  Anyone who wants a bit,
  I'll acquit myself, you bet!

FIRST DEMON

> Come on, off to our temple!
> The tyrant king says he will
> sacrifice now!
> He's out to do evil deeds –
> a quick look is all we need.
> It won't help him anyhow!

[The demons descend to the temple]

TYRANT KING

> Come into the temple, come!
> Our god is not a simple one.
> All honour to him is due!

[all genuflect]

> Here's a white-necked bull's head,
> I offer it with due dread.
> Take! I am your servant true.

FIRST TORTURER

> I shall not let my god down!
> Here's a ram's head, O Mahound,
> I've gilded the horns – it shows.
> My present should suit you well –
> it has a fine pungent smell,
> so I'll set it by your nose.

SECOND TORTURER

> I've a horse's head for you,
> please take and keep that, too,
> a worthy prize!
> It's an extremely fine piece
> worth ten quid or so at least,
> and a fine sight for your eyes.

THIRD TORTURER

> To my god, Jove the benign,
> three ravens I here assign,
> marvellously formed, I'd say.
> They are worth a bob or two,
> and I got them all for you
> on horseback, from far away.

CALO (THE TYRANT KING'S SKIVVY)

> To Jove my god, directly,
> here is a tomcat from me,
> the best mouser you could find.
> I bought him down in Morville
> where the devil lives in hell.
> Let him take all from my hand:
> a goat's head, one skinned as well,
> my god, our service is kind!

[They all sing]

FIRST DEMON

> Left-handed blessings on you!
> Evil and nastiness too,
> use them by choice!
> Make sure you steal from the poor;
> the curses that on you pour
> will make your spirits rejoice.

FIRST TORTURER

> Now on our way we may go.
> Our Holy-Father-Below
> to us has sent
> his benediction and law,
> to go forth and rob the poor
> and this is his commandment.

SECOND TORTURER

> I've got a great itching in
> my hands to commit a sin!
> So let us go!
> If we can find a traitor
> or any malefactor,
> we'll get him – we won't be slow!

THIRD TORTURER

> Who cares where we head for now?
> We'll not be back anyhow!
> "People seek us everywhere,
> even those nearest and dear,
> but we'll keep ourselves well clear
> and we'll never have a care!

[They all leave]

Religious Parody

This parody of the liturgy comes from a manuscript of the fifteenth century which is now in the Palatine Library in Rome, with a parallel manuscript in Halberstadt. Of German origin, it is one of very many different Latin versions, just as there are plenty of parodies of prayers, the Psalms and even the Gospels. There is similar material in the *Carmina Burana*. The various elements play upon actual introits and familiar prayers, with Bacchus, god of drink, and Decius, god of the dice, taking over the main parts. Puns like *leccator*, 'scrounger, crook' or *potator*, 'drinker,' for *peccator* 'sinner,' and *omnipotans* 'all-drinking' instead of *omnipotens*, 'all-powerful' are predictably tricky to translate, and imitation is the best one can hope for.

The Drinkers' Mass

LET US confess to Lord Bacchus, inasmuch as he is good, and inasmuch as in goblets and tankards is his great potability. For I am a wretch, and I have conned.

CONFITEOR. Therefore do I make confession to Naughty Bacchus and all Tankards, and in the sight of all of you drinkers, that I, a drinker weak, have drunk to excess in my life, drinking whilst sitting, drinking whilst throwing dice, drinking whilst invoking the name of Christ Almighty, yea, gambling away my shirt. My most grievous sin, my most grievous sin. Therefore do I implore ye, O my brothers in drink, that ye imbibe with me, a drinker, to Naughty Bacchus in his infinite Wine-vat, that he may have mercy upon me, a poor drinker.

MAY THE LORD Bacchus in his infinite Wineskin have mercy upon thee, and may he lead thee into the hostelry of the blessed, that thou mayst lose thy shirt, thy teeth and also thine eyes, and that thou mayst no longer walk nor feel thy hands. For this is the malediction of the Unholy Dice, which doth afflict the spirit. Which drinketh and slurpeth from boozer to boozer, pissed without end.

Bar-men.

MAY THE LORD Bacchus, who boozeth and reigneth in discord and in wretchedness, visit upon thee indigence, dissoluteness, delusion, perdition, and great persistence without any hope of winning, even unto the loss of the shirt off thy back, yea, even thine underpants, through his most Unholy Dice.

Bar-men.

Booze be with us in the name of Bacchus, who did create Tavern and Jug.

INTROIT. Let us all cry out to him, filled with mild-and-bitterness, with weeping and lamentations for the failings of the cubed and vengeful Dice, through the throwing of which the impoverished are caused to weep and blaspheme in the name of Christ.

PSALM. Blessed are those who dwell in thy Taverns, O Bacchus, for they shall laud thee from boozer to boozer. Yet to me shall come no glory, for lo! my purse is empty.

Piss-ups be with you.
And with thy spirituous liquors.

LET US DRINK. O Lord, who has rewarded three rolling dice with sixty-three spots, we beseech thee to grant that all who wish to place their shirts thereupon, that they, by the throwing of these dice, be fleecèd. Through the most holy wines-and-spirits of our grandfather Bacchus, who inbibeth and guzzleth with us from boozer to boozer, pissed without end.

Bar-men.

THE LESSON. From the Epissed-all to the Home-brews. My brothers, in those days there was in the tavern a great multitude of drinkers, and their bodies were naked, having no shirts. And there was not one amongst them that had a thing he could call his own, for verily they were all in it together.

And those amongst them that were possessed of the price of a drink, verily, they were held with honour in the sight of the drinkers. And there was with them in those days a certain legless one, and his name was called Boozi, which signifieth a slob of the worst sort. And he had amassed unto himself much lucre, causing great indebtedness amongst the peoples. And he gaveth unto the drinkers there assembled a reason for dicing and imbibing, inasmuch as they set great store by keeping their shirts.

GRADUAL. Cast thy thoughts unto the Unholy Dice, and it shall deceive thee. For this is the work of the bottle, and it doeth great wonders unto our purses.

ALLLELUIA. Halitosis. In my cups did I drink even unto leglessness, and the Unholy Dice undid me. Hail, O tosis.

SEQUENCE. Wine with a nose is good for you,
the abbot drinks it and the prior too,
in a crowd or with just a few,
stops you being sad.

Here's to the liquor, jolly good stuff,
water of life and that's enough,
every bar-counter's smooth, not rough,
prop it up, my lad.

Lucky old belly when the wine goes in,
lucky old you when it wets your chin,
lucky old tongue slopping over him,
makes your lips feel glad.

O how warm is its appeal,
O how the fire is truly real,
O how good it makes you feel,
if you're sloshed, too bad!

Let us pray: give us it neat,
makes all our racketing sound sweet,
joyous voices then all meet,
praising with a roar.

Let the monks come in a crowd,
clergy! everyone's allowed,
let us drink and sing out loud
now and evermore.

GOSPEL. May the booze be with you. And with your wines-and-spirits. The reading is from the Gospel according to Bacchus, to whom be Glory, Fraud and Horror.

In their daze, the drinkers spake amongst themselves, saying: 'Let us go forth even unto the tavern and see for ourselves whether those words be true which the good landlord hath told us of a land flowing with mild and bitter. And entering therefore the tavern, they made haste towards the tabernacles of the host, who did spread a table in their sight, and there were goblets upon it. And drinking, therefore, they did acknowledge Bacchus and saw that what he had told them of the contents of the barrels was true. And the good landlord did reckon up in his heart what value these men might place upon their shirts. And when that they were rat-arsed, then did he divide them from their garments. And lo, the drinkers returned again to their own dwelling-places glorifying and praising Bacchus and cursing the name of Dice.
For is it not written in the Gospels? And if a man falleth into the ditch, so shall that be tough luck on him.

OFFERTORY. Hangovers be with you. And with thy D.T.s. O Bacchus, most mighty of drinkers, who bringeth forth stupidity out of the wise and evil out of the good, fill us now with thine insobriety and tarry not!

PREFACE. From boozer to boozer. Bar-men. Thickness be in your heads. And up thine, buddy. I shall raise my hopes in the Unholy Dice. Let us give thanks to Naughty Bacchus, our help in vintages past.

For merrily I say unto thee, in the imbibing of his infinite wine-bar is our salutation. Therefore ought we to give thanks and praise, bless and preach the good wines in his taverns. For that they are swilled by the poorest peasant; and for that they are drunk by noble lords and clerics; and for that they are adored by priests; and for that they are of great price; and for that they may be supped to satisfaction; and for that they restore health and strength unto a man, causing the wretched to laugh, the clergy to sing, and the inebriates to chant without ceasing day by day in one voice, saying:
Lovely, lovely, lovely, Lord Bacchus of Mine-Hosts. The tankards and bars are filled with thy glory. Hosanna in excesses. Cursed be he who drinketh the shirt off his own back. Pollyanna sex in Chelsea.
From boozer to boozer. Bar-men.

LET US DRINK. For the good landlord taught us to drink good wines, saying: OUR BACCHUS, which art in tankards, swallowed be thy wine. Thy kingdom come. Thy wildness be done, with dice as it is in taverns. Give us this day our daily booze, and forgive us our pissartistry as we forgive them that welsh upon us. Lead us not into good company, but deliver us from our cash. Bar-men.

From boozer to boozer. Bar-men.

Sods be with you. And may the fraud-squad have mercy.
O Slob of Bacchus, who taketh away the sobriety of the world, give us a drop. O Slob of wine, who owneth the pub of the world, give us our drink.

O Slob of Slobs, who taketh away our last halfpenny, give us thy pint.

COMMUNION. Come, O ye children of Bacchus and look upon the booze which he hath prepared for you from the beginning of time. Hangovers shall be with you.

And with thy D.T.s.

LET US QUAFF: O God of Wine, who soweth perpetual discord between the clergy and the peasants, and who hath caused many of the peasantry to plunge into penury and indebtedness, grant we beseech thee now and forever that we may live off them and abuse their wives and children and rejoice at their downfall. In the name of our slurred Bacchus, who imbibeth and raveth from boozer to boozer, pissed without end. Bar-men.

May the fraud-squad be with thee.
Ite, piss-up est. For it is opening time. Thanks be to Bacchus.
Amazing liquor, how smooth thy taste, for through thy grace is a layman made into a lawyer, a monk into an abbot and a peasant into a pillock. For I came even unto his boozer and I tarried not.

Preaching About Blue Ducks

Thomas Murner (1475–1537) was one of Martin Luther's opponents (and a vigorous one – see the next piece!), but in fact he anticipated some of his reforms. A Franciscan with a lively eye for abuse, he attacked a range of follies in the *Guild of Fools* in 1512, much in the style of Brant's *Ship of Fools*. Here Murner has a go at populist preachers who waste time on nonsense. If the choice of 'blue ducks' as a nonsense theme seems a bit odd, it is because the German word for 'ducks' – *Enten* – rhymes with theological words like 'sacraments' or 'Testaments.' The English word 'duck' is unfortunate in that potential rhymes are, well, unfortunate.

Thomas Murner

The Guild of Fools

'I am the first one in this herd,
because I mock God's holy word.
When I proclaim God's mystery
I do it very flippantly,
as if the Christians I'd confuse,
and 'blue ducks' is the theme I choose.
Odds guts! Odds bodikins! I swear
that preacher would be quite unfair
who threw the Bible in my face
on matters of the soul or grace;
no, let him tell a joke instead,
or some news that he's lately read,
and laugh and joke us out of hell.
Since all the priests join in as well
and make what's serious a game,
I reckon I'll just do the same!
I find God's word as serious
as chewing on a piece of grass,
and that's as long as it will last.'

When God's word is my heart's desire,
they read me Bulls about hell-fire,
or news of John or Jack or Jill,
or who's refused to pay some bill,
or how the towns of such and such
are fighting over nothing much,
or all about some local fair,
or at the dance, what you should wear.
But when I want to hear God's word
I hear this rubbish – it's absurd –
people shouting each other down
as loud as fishwives in the town.
Each calls the next a liar and more;
instead of Gospels, we get war
up in the pulpit in God's sight!
Now, is that pious? Is that right?
They are supposed to teach us things –
but all we get is arguing,
and they distort all God's teaching.

The damage they do is far-reaching
when 'blue ducks' is their theme for preaching.

Thomas Murner and the Protestants

Unlike the last piece, the ideas of which are quite close to Luther's, this one is an attack on him. Protestants like Ruf had criticised a Catholic Church run by such morally suspect (if art-loving, not to say fun-loving) families as the Borgias or the Medicis, but Catholicism saw the reformers as a decadent lot, because they threw out most of the sacraments and thereby gave licence, it was claimed, to unrestricted vice. Murner was a sharp enemy because he focussed on genuine details of Protestant doctrine, accusing them of using their insistence on the Scriptures only when they could find Biblical justification for smashing monasteries and general mayhem. In this huge work – nearly five thousand lines – the Great Fool is the Reformation, with Luther as a little fool in its belly. Murner adopts the role the Protestant polemicists gave him, that of *Murr-Narr*, the 'Tomcat-Fool' (*Murr* is a name for a cat in German and *Narr* means fool), and has Luther offer him his daughter in marriage. Accepting Luther's wonderfully lax doctrines, Murner marries her, but then rejects her because she has a revolting skin disease, and marriage isn't a sacrament anyway. Luther dies, and because extreme unction has also been scrapped, he is dumped in the privy, while a cats' chorus supplants the last rites.

Thomas Murner

On The Great Lutheran Fool

Luther explains Protestantism to Murner (lines 3746–3904)

LUTHER

> Well, since I find you of a mind
> and to my daughter well inclined,
> I'd better tell you how you can
> turn into a good Lutheran.
> In fact, I think I'll write it down

241

so my views can be spread around
to men and women in the town,
and everyone will understand
the new doctrines that we have planned,
and so our Lutherosity
can be maintained more easily.
The first rule that we have devised
is that the Pope must be despised
(he is the devil's spawn from hell!)
then bishops must be mocked as well,
and all the clergy and the priests
(the devil spawned them too, the beasts,
and he imbued them with his vice).
The Pope's also the Antichrist,
because the geese in Germany
never elected him, you see?
I know his crown is triple, but
one is too many for that mutt!
And as for all his Papal Bulls,
the silly, vicious, impious fool,
enforced by legates double-quick
(he really is a massive prick!),
we'll trample on them straight away,
and we won't fast, confess or pray.
We will not recognise his writ,
we'll make a bonfire out of it,
and we shall do the same, what's more,
for the Holy Roman Emperor,
the princes and all the estates,
the Emperor's associates.
If this lot promulgates a law,
that's one we'll take care to ignore.
The laws that they try to impose,
we'll laugh and spit at all of those.
We won't keep anything they say,
or care about it anyway,
for Christian Faith makes us all free
to reject all authority.

Baptism frees us all today,
so kings and princes have no say.
Now, Lutheran rule number three
is to reject the liturgy.
The Mass? The devil thought of it
and it won't help us, not a bit,
neither in life, nor afterward.
A mass is an insult to God,
a piece of loathsome frippery
to rob us all dishonestly
of all our Lutherosity.
The Mass can't be a sacrifice,
the Gospel shown by artifice;
don't water wine in the chalice.
Confession we don't need at all
unless it's between two good pals.
Confirming, marriage, the Last Rites?
throw the whole lot out of our sight,
never let them come to light!
If to be Lutheran you yearn,
for every sacrament you'll turn –
that's what Luther makes us learn!
Smash up each church and monastery,
slash every icon that you see,
the sacraments must be debased
and nuns out of their convents chased,
and monks out of the monastery –
do that, if Lutheran you'd be.
If like a Lutheran you'd preach,
the monks and priests you must impeach,
and mock the clergy near and far
to show how Lutheran you are,
that you speak truth, open and free,
and be everyone's enemy.
Whatever monks once did of yore,
bring it all up and to the fore,
and talk about their luxury
(but *not* about their piety).

To dredge up every little bit
that there has ever been of shit
is what everyone has to do
(just so that they'll stink of it, too).
Those wicked arguments that man
has had since Christendom began,
and which have long since, far and wide,
by Christian men been set aside –
revive the lot! Bring back the schism!
We don't want all this pacifism.
Yes, that's our spirit and our mood,
we'll wash our hands in pools of blood,
and wade in it up to the knee –
now that's real Lutherosity!
Cultivate lies carefully
but truth must be claimed publicly;
just say that what *we* say holds good,
but other folk trot out falsehood.
If you should find us lying, too,
we always claim that it is true,
the very Gospel, nothing false,
that's what it has to be, of course.
And keep it quiet, furthermore,
that we've got weaponry in store
(so we can rob the priests, you see,
more quickly and more easily).
We'll take their cash and gold away,
the priests have plenty anyway.
We'll damn the bishops merrily,
and we'll nick all their property,
then let the merchants have their turn,
and take away the cash they earn
(like those in Prague just had to learn –
yes, their town council had enough
when we took all the merchants' stuff,
we stole whatever we could find
and didn't leave a scrap behind).
But let me shorten what I've said

and summarise the rules instead:
just keep this thought inside your head –
anger and malice are our creed,
they burn within us, yes indeed!
When someone's better off than we,
our one desire has to be
to take it off him, every groat,
and then to get him by the throat,
take all his goods into our hands,
and after, raze his house and lands
and torch the lot and watch it burn –
that's the way of a Lutheran!
Well now, enough doctrine, my friend,
my set of rules is at an end –
just turn everything inside out,
and that's our Gospel, without doubt;
so there is what you have to do
if you would be Lutheran too.
If you see all things upside-down,
leave the fire for the frying pan,
if a baby craps when at the font
we know that he's the one we want!
We call them 'Children of Mayhem,'
and that's the Lutheran order, then,
which is observed by Luther's men.
You mustn't go to church too much,
or use the Book of Hours and such.
Well, Murner, I've spelt out to you
what our order demands you do,
and if by our rules you will live,
then gladly my daughter I'll give.
Is your answer affirmative?

MURNER

Odds bodikins, this is good stuff,
your rules all seem easy enough.
If they're the rules that you avow,
I'd be at least abbot by now . . .

MURNER

> Out, out! In every devil's name,
> by whose force we together came!
> You scruffy monk's whore, ratbag, clown!
> Out, out! May thunder strike you down.
> If you are Luther's sweet child true,
> how can you be so poxy, too?
> You stink the room out totally,
> and want to go to bed with *me*?
> Out, out! Clear off! It's very plain
> I don't want to see you again!
> If I should find you, I declare
> that I shall flay you, that I swear!
> You slagheap, poxy pile of stink,
> you slut! How could you even think
> that ever by my side you'd lie?
> Go to the sows in the pigsty!

LUTHER

> Hang on a minute, Murner, hey!
> Why are you hitting her that way,
> driving my daughter from your door
> with blows and curses? What's it for?
> They warned me you would really be
> a trial, and how you'd repay me!
> Before my friends you've brought me shame
> who, in my honour, kindly came
> to share this spicy wedding-feast!
> Have you become some kind of beast
> to beat my daughter on the bum
> out here in front of everyone?

MURNER

> Take my advice, hear what I say,
> and keep your daughter well away,
> or else I'll never be your friend.
> That ratbag's poxed from end to end –
> one sniff of her and you can tell,

246

so take the brat, and go to hell!
Besides, you told me your intent,
that marriage be no sacrament.
If it's a sacrament no more
well then, I've done no wrong, I'm sure.
Rascals and whores, divorce at will
the minute you have had your fill!
If to no sacrament I'm true,
well, piss on her and piss on you!
Just look at her – her poxy sores
are thicker than a sow's, and more!
They're thicker than a tinker's cough,
so take the slut and bugger off!

Luther dies of shock and Murner arranges a burial (4414–76)

MURNER
A burial reflects the worth
a man had when he lived on earth.
The one thing Luther did down here
for peaceful Christendom, I fear,
was bring us schism and the sword,
and now he's reaped evil's reward.
Off to the shit-house with the chap
who said the sacraments were crap –
send him off with a thunderclap!
The shit-house is the place for such
as leave no scrap of filth untouched.

HOW LUTHER'S BURIAL WAS HYMNED WITH A MIGHTY
CATERWAULING

From Luther's teaching I deduce
that Holy Mass is not much use
in death or in our life on earth,
and for damned souls has damn-all worth.

. . .

Of other details I'm not sure,
but I'll be kind to Pa-in-Law

247

and we at least shall sing something,
and all the cats together bring.
A cat is what *they've* made of me
(and not behaved too courteously)
remember though, touch not the cat!

But if I asked them after that
to Luther's requiem today,
the cats would make them stay away,
which would insult me anyway,
and that would be a great disgrace
and I should lose a lot of face.

Therefore, my pussies, jump up higher
and *we* shall make a funeral choir,
we cats will sing around the pyre.
I shall start off, and you join in,
and keep it low, lads, no screeching,
just stay in tune, I beg you all,
and let's not have a caterwaul.
Come black cats, grey cats, anyhow,
and sing miaow, miaow, miaow,
miaow, miaow – keep singing too,
for Murn–iaow, the Tomcat-Fool.
Mew, mew, the tenors to the fore,
miaow, miaow, bass in the score.
Now if I'm *not* a pussy-cat,
how come I can miaow like that?
So now it's clear by what great rule
they call me–iaow the Tomcat-Fool.
I can miaow with such fine tone
and sing that Pa-in-Law has gone,
and not leave him to lie alone.
If cats had not answered my call
he'd have no requiem at all . . .

EPILOGUE: LAMENTS FOR A MISSPENT YOUTH

Living a life of wickedness is never really a problem while one is actually *doing* it. It is not death that is the wages of sin, but old age and attendant debility. This section includes expressions of the problem from the point of view of men and women (though the writers were probably all men). The male-voice pieces are pretty specific about the parts which fail to operate; the one in a woman's voice is more generally elegaic.

Just as there is a long tradition of poetry addressed to the over-active penis (as with Dafydd ap Gwilym), there is also a poetry of complaint about its inactivity which goes back to Ovid's temporary failure in the *Amores*, and has a famous post-medieval expression in the poetry of the Earl of Rochester (as well as in a soldiers' song about a water-spout). It isn't always old age that causes the problem. This first short text is from a German manuscript of the early fifteenth century, and it was printed by Lassberg (who supplied the title) in the 1820s with an apologetic note for including it at all, and pleading that it was strictly of linguistic interest. The second piece on a similar theme is by the Scottish poet Sir Duncan Campbell, who was born in 1443 and died at Flodden in 1513. Several Gaelic poems are attributed to him. He had a go at priests, and wrote a long and rather adjectival boast to his penis, much as Dafydd ap Gwilym did. He was also acutely aware of its failure, though one can only wonder about his wife and her reaction.

249

What shall I do? It's pretty poor!
I can't raise Willy any more!
He droops and dangles there today,
and won't respond in any way
to all the ladies that I see,
and just hangs, detumescently!
He thinks he'll stay there, limp and small,
and he's got the idea that all
he'll do is flop maliciously –
why should he act so viciously!
He's started mocking everyone,
pisses on shoes (he thinks that's fun!),
pees down your trousers, makes a mess,
he's really like a stinking cess-
pit, pongs a lot, but doesn't twitch.
As habits go, it's quite a bitch!

A lady pilgrim, off to Rome
should not forget my balls, back home.
So let no lady's eyes distress,
just let her bathe them in this piss,
and they won't hurt her any more.

If Willy plumbed deep lakes before,
well, let's recall that, and rejoice,
'cause now he droops without a choice!

Duncan Campbell of Glenorchy

Poem VI

Bad luck to him whose manly powers wane,
    the sadness of it occupies my mind.
Think well on what has now become of me,
    make sure you have no truck with womankind!

When I was younger, for a little while
    I would enjoy myself in every way;
before my manly powers started to
    malfunction, I was happy every day.

But now, alas, my comforts are no more
    a great change, sadly, has come over me.
I had the taste of honey all the time
    until I lost my male vitality.

Once (and quite properly) I drank the lot,
    not one wine, red or white, beneath the sun
did I miss out, but sampled them as well.
    It didn't last though, and those times are done.

So there's my problem now, the one I mean,
    it's plain enough for anyone to see:
as long as I still had my vigour, then
    there was a full share of good things for me.

My wife! Good God, she's worse than all the rest,
    now that I've come to be in this bad way.
She won't stop nagging, scolding, bullying,
    and just keeps at it (and me) every day.

Once there was no exotic food or spice
    nor any kind of fine and tasty fish
beneath the sun that would not come my way,
    to satisfy each culinary wish.

And while John Thomas had his health and strength,
    the sweetest fruit you'd find in your whole life
was waiting for me three times every day
    at least, provided by my own young wife.

If I had told her then that God was just
    an ordinary chap, or goats were swine,
well, she'd agree with everything I said,
    even if I claimed water to be wine.

But now, if I should offer her the moon
    and stars, and everything there is to see,
now that John T. has ceased to function, she'll
    just say: 'No thanks. You can't do much for me!'

If all the heroes in the world were mine
    to order, from the earth and oceans wide,
from east to west, it still would be no good;
    my wife would still never be satisfied.

Sweet Jesus Christ, I beg you, hear my plea,
    as you are king of every church, and mine,
please grant my willy everlasting strength,
    so I can try to keep my wife in line.

Other great men, nobles and fighters all,
    rampaged and ravaged lands from sea to sea –
then waned! The terra incognita where
    they went must – sadly – now be home to me.

Life at the Ebb

The speaker in this very famous Old Irish poem, written probably in around 900 (opinions differ), doesn't *regret* her wanton life – she thoroughly enjoyed it, in fact, making love and drinking far into the night. Now life is ebbing, though, and she has to come to terms with being an old woman, resentful that everything in nature seems to survive better than humans. She may be a nun, but no-one is really sure about that, or many other aspects of the text.

The Lady of Beare, Grown Old

Ebbing I am, like the tide.
   Ageing has yellowed me.
Though I may rage at the pain,
   age comes on greedily.

I am the Lady of Beare, grown
   old. Once I wore a new gown
daily. Today I hardly own
   more than one reach-me-down.

It's gold
you love now, not folk!
   In our day, back then,
   what *we* loved was men.

The men whose lands we roved
   we loved the most.
They were fine hosts to us,
   and afterwards made no boasts.

Now, bragging is what they do best.
   What they *don't* do is provide.
They give little, keep the rest,
   and put on a lot of side.

Chariots, speed,
and the very fastest steeds –
    there were plenty of them then.
And glory for the king's deeds!

My body – it's all bitterness today –
can't wait to reach that well-known place.
    When the Son of God decrees,
let Him come and lead me away.

My arms! Look at them now –
    scrawny, bony things!
Once they were better used,
    embracing great kings.

Scrawny, bony arms –
    look at them now. I'm sure
they'll never clasp
    a young man any more.

Young girls are full of joy
    when Spring comes and the sun's gold.
I'm not just sad.
    Worse: I'm a woman, and I'm *old*.

Too late for speeches,
    no fatted calf for my wedding fare.
My hair is thin and grey,
    and I cover it, and I don't care.

I wear a thick veil now,
but it makes no difference anyhow.
    My head-dresses were bright and fine
    back when we drank the best wine.

I envy no-one, just the fields
of corn at Feimen, and their yield.

254

Years have finished me. But that plain
will be gold with corn again.

The Standing Stone of the Kings,
the great Stone House – these things
    are lashed for years by storms,
    and yet *they're* not age-worn.

The waves crash noisily
on Winter's high sea.
    No king's son, not even a slave
    will visit me across those waves.

I know what they are doing,
  . where they are today;
the ones that might have come
    sleep in the cold clay.

Sad for me
that I no longer sail youth's sea.
    My years of beauty are all gone
    and my days of lust done.

Bad for me
that however fine the day be,
    I must wrap up well, even in the heat.
    Cold age is the great threat.

Summer of youth is for us all.
I had it, and then fall.
    Winter of age gets everyone.
    I have it. Its first months have come.

Well, youth's summer was well-spent.
    I enjoyed it where I could.
There's not much more to go now,
    but no regrets. It was good.

The fields are rich and green:
   God's cloak lies over Drummain,
spread by the one great king –
   rough earth made smooth again.

Yes, yes, I am cold.
   All things are born to decay.
I used to feast in bright halls.
   Now I kneel in the dark to pray.

Once I had my day with kings,
drinking wine and feasting,
   now I drink watered milk
beside withered old women.

Well, let me drink watered milk,
   that's no sin.
But let the living God
   calm the rage that burns within.

The cloak of life is frayed today,
my rambling mind leads me astray,
   the grey hairs which grow on me
   are like the bark of a rotting tree.

My right eye has lost its light
by God's law; but heaven is in sight.
   The left eye dims too.
   My inner sight is heaven's view.

Three floods
engulf Ard Ruide:
   flood of horses, flood of men
   flood of hounds swift as the wind.

Flood-wave,
   and the ebb comes then.
What the flood-wave brings,

the ebb carries off again.

Flood-wave,
  and the ebb comes to the shore.
I've known them all. I have
  seen what will come no more.

Flood-wave,
but my cell's like the silent grave.
  All my many folk are in the dark,
a cold hand on them laid.

I suppose Holy Christ knew
  I'd need the help of Mary's son.
How generous was I in my time?
  Well, I never said 'no' to any one!

It's grave
that man is so depraved,
  that we can't see the ebb
when we ride the high flood-wave.

My flood-wave
  kept its secrets thoroughly.
What Jesus, Mary's son reveals
  at ebb, that doesn't trouble me.

An island standing in the ocean wide,
after each ebb gets another flood-tide.
  I'm no island. There cannot be
  a fresh flood-tide of youth for me.

When I look at places,
  there's nowhere I recognise today.
What was flood-tide once
  is ebbing away.

The originals of most of the earlier theological and historical selections may be found in the massive (and heavy) compilations of the nineteenth century. Migne's *Patrologia Latina* (Paris, 1844–64) has Gregory the Great; the *Monumenta Germaniae Historica* (Weimar, 1832–) has *Waltharius*, Gregory of Tours, the *Cambridge Songs* (including the Snow-Baby), Einhard, Nithard; the *Rolls Series* (London) has Matthew Paris, the *Annales Paulini*, Thomas de la Moore, William of Newburgh and Ranulph Higden. Much of the vernacular literature is also found in the text-series begun around the end of the last century: the *Early English Text Society* has the books of manners (under the title of *The Babees Book*) and Andrew Boorde; the *Altdeutsche Textbibliothek* (published in Halle and then Tübingen) has *Helmbrecht*; the Leipzig *Deutsche Literatur in Entwicklungsreihen* has the works of Thomas Murner; the *Classiques français du moyen age* (Paris) include Rutebeuf. Ruf's play is in an older series, the *Bibliothek der deutschen Nationalliteratur* (Leipzig). The play of Meriasek was edited and translated by Whitley Stokes (London, 1872). H. J. Schmitz, *Die Bußbücher und die Bußdisziplin der Kirche* (Mainz, 1883) has the *Corrector*, H. F. Massmann published the Forms of Confession in 1839, and the mock-mass is in Paul Lehmann's *Die Parodie in Mittelalter* (repr. Stuttgart, 1963). The full horrors of Gilles de Rais are in Latin in Eugène Bossard, *Gilles de Rais* (Paris, 2. ed. 1886) and there is a French version of it all by Georges Battaille, *Le procès de Gilles de Rais* (Montreuil, 1965). There are many editions of Froissart (and the Bourchier translation) and of Boccaccio (older versions of the Everyman edition have our story in Italian). A full edition of the various versions of the *Anglo-Saxon Chronicle* is in progress, but there are several nineteenth century Clarendon editions. Lassberg's *Liedersaal*, from which the German impotence-poem was taken, appeared in the early nineteenth century, but has been reprinted, and the Sidgwick anthology, one of the many places in which the 'gentle cock' has crowed, first appeared in 1907. The originals of Cecco's poems can be found in anthologies such as the *Penguin Book of Italian Verse;* there is a diplomatic version of the whole Codex Karlsruhe (which has the 'Monk and Goose' story as well as the Adam and Eve sermon) edited by U. Schmid (Berne and Munich, 1974), and the standard edition of the *Carmina Burana* is that by A. Hilka, O. Schumann and B. Bischoff published in Heidelberg between 1930 and 1970. There is a truncated edition of Dafydd ap Gwilym's poem in the edition of Peniarth 49 by T. Parry (Cardiff, 1929), but for a fuller text see David Johnston's in *Cambridge Medieval Celtic Studies* 9 (1985), pp. 71–89. The poems of Duncan Campbell are edited with a prose version by William Gillies (*Scottish Gaelic Studies* 13, 1978–81, pp. 18–45 and 263–88 and 14, 1983, 59–82). For *The Old Woman of Beare* see my paper in the *Zeitschrift für celtische Philologie* 44 (1991), pp. 80–127.